Circulate Bo

C000036677

My Memoirs from The Oil Industry

by Craig Douglas

Acknowledgement

It is not everyone who has the opportunity to write about their career adventures - in my case, memoirs from the oil industry. Racking my brains about what has all happened over the years has been an enjoyable experience, but I do wonder if the Covid - 19 pandemic had never arrived if I would ever have found, or made, the time to write these memoirs.

I want to thank my wife, Judith, for listening to me whittering on while writing this book, on top of all the years of understanding and support. I should also apologise to Judith, as well as our children, Amy and Iain, for taking them to Qatar as part of my adventures. Thankfully both Amy and Iain were too young to fully understand what was going on at the time.

I would like to thank Judith's good friend Pat Dogan (nee Miller) for putting the idea into my head and getting me started on this project. Also, Mark 'Taffy' Jones for his company and assistance when we both started out in the industry all those years ago.

To my good friend David Knox for deciphering my ramblings and editing them into a readable form. To a friend I dearly miss, Bernard Halford - the former Manchester City Secretary and Life President. Bernard is no longer with us but when I suggested a few years ago, that he should write a book about his 50 years in football he declined, suggesting, as modestly as ever, that my stories from the oil industry would be every bit as interesting. That is something I doubt very much. Bernard would never shift on the idea of a book, mainly because of the fear of wandering around a car boot sale on a Sunday and seeing his biography for sale at 50 pence. It's such a pity he is no longer here to read this.

To rig manager Donald Millar, who I feel I have now known for a lifetime and a day. Donald has been of great assistance with this project. As has Eddie McWilliams with his input and assistance. One of the highlights of my job is meeting Eddie in Edinburgh for post project meetings. Those few hours of drinking and reminiscing always pass very quickly. To Darryl Fury, who has been a loyal instructor and good friend. To Alexander 'Barker' Bruce - where would JCD Training ever have been regarding scaffold training without the Barker? His input into the dates where we all were, and the memories has been an immense help in compiling this book.

To QHSE manager Stuart Meachen (now retired) for his help all those years ago when I first started in business. Stuart's input has always been well received. To Stuart Bowler for refreshing my memory on everything that occurred in Vietnam all those years ago. And to Jim Stamford for his memories of Mermaid Drilling and the MTR1 and 2.

And to everyone else who has help make the past thirty years such an adventure.

Foreword

After working all over the world in the oil industry since 1987, it was suggested by one of my wife's close friends that it was perhaps time to put pen to paper and write about my stories and times in the industry. As she kindly said, 'Once you go, all these stories will be lost forever'. To protect identities I have occasionally changed some names.

To an outsider this may be an unusual title for a book but to anyone who has worked on the drill floor of an oil rig, I'm sure they will agree that it was somewhat of a relief to go on shift at midnight as a roughneck and find out the 'well was circulating bottoms up'. The term involves using mud to clean an unfinished well or get rid of any unwanted gases coming back up.

The highs and the lows of 33 years in the industry are detailed in this memoir, including my family's terrible experience in Qatar, where instead of coming back to the UK a multimillionaire, I was lucky to get out of the country in one piece - not just myself but also my wife and two children. I discuss the experiences of Singapore and other zones as well as the pressures of a job where when oil prices are high you can be the flavour of the month with a client, to the next the very opposite. My time was most often spent working in West Africa, South America and South East Asia where I had the pleasure of actually being paid to visit places like Thailand, Malaysia, Indonesia and Vietnam. I've enjoyed the oil industry, as you're about to read, and I hope you enjoy *Circulate Bottoms Up*.

Countries where JCD Training has conducted training

Angola

Australia

Argentina

Brunei

China

Denmark

Egypt

East Timor

Equatorial Guinea

Gabon

Ghana

Japan

Iran

Indonesia

Ivory Coast

Malaysia

Myanmar

Nigeria

Netherlands

Norway

Qatar

Republic of Congo

Romania

Saudi Arabia

Singapore

South Korea

Thailand

Tunisia

Trinidad

United Arab Emirates

United Kingdom

Vietnam

Types of Oil Rigs

Platform

Once oil has been discovered, a platform will be built by an oil company to acts as a fixed installation where the oil can be extracted.

Semi Submersible Drilling Rig

An exploration rig that floats on pontoons when on location, with water flooded into the pontoons to act alongside anchors, enabling the rig to drill.

Drill Ship

Used for deep sea drilling

Jack Up Drilling Rig

Once on location, the legs of jack up drilling rigs are jacked down to seabed. Huge spud cans attached to the base of the legs are filled with water to allow stability for drilling to begin.

Drill Assist Tender Barge

These barges are floated beside usually small platforms and have no drilling capabilities or accommodation for personnel. It is only once a tender barge is rigged up, with drilling packages, etc, that it can drill or conduct other work. Once the contract is finished, all packaging is retrieved and the barge moves to another location.

Disciplines onboard a drilling rig

OIM (Offshore Installation Manager)

Tool Pusher

Driller

Asst Driller

Derrick man

Assistant Derrick man

Roughneck (Floor man)

Crane Operator

Assistant Crane Operator

Roustabout

Marine Crew

First Mate (Night Captain)

Barge Engineer

Chief Engineer

Rig Mechanic

Sub Sea Engineer

Hydraulic Engineer

Rig Electrician

Motor man (Oiler)

Dyvi Stena Personnel

These are the people I had the pleasure of meeting and working with, between 1987 and 1991, on board Dyvi Stena. Unfortunately, some of these guys are not with us any longer. My apologies if someone has been missed out.

Ron Sturrock	Helge Tosse
Stan Preston	Tony Simmons
Steve Zaroletta	Andy Dickinson
Jimmy Walker	Gavin Severn
Malcolm McRitchie	John McMillan
Neil Massie	Ian Davidson (Odd Job)
Jim Donald	Tony Lambert
Alex McAulay	Uisdean McLean
Iain Boyd	
John Beaumont	
Alan Salah	
Gerry Edwards	
Steve Grant	
Dougie Henderson	
Fred Wylie	
Alex (Minty) Reid	
Alex Smith	
Davie Davidson	
Rudy Mueller	
David Smitz Muller	

John Norrie

Les Law

John Eveleigh

Peter Armstrong

Chapter 1

Montrose, Scotland: 1986
Where it all began

From a young age I had always wanted to get into the oil industry but found it a hard nut to crack. Coming from Selkirk in the Scottish Borders also complicated matters, as the distance to the oil capital of Aberdeen is considerable. An old friend of a friend who was also originally from Selkirk and a good deal older than me, had managed it and did okay working a 28/28 rotation (twenty-eight days on, twenty-eight days off) or as we say month on, month off. Unfortunately, he kept his cards close to his chest and getting him to show me through the door was verging on impossible. He made plenty money, coming home every month in the late 1970s early 80s with US $5,000. He was working on an old Jack-up drilling rig offshore in the Persian Gulf, with the crew changing out of Abu Dhabi in the United Arab Emirates. He made it to Driller, which is not bad a position. He even used to get an air ticket to a chosen destination at the end of his hitch instead of flying home to UK. Not bad a deal at all. I wanted some of that.

I remember once almost getting a job as a steward in the North Sea with a catering company, but at around eighteen or nineteen I was too young. The guy from Selkirk who did get the job was sacked for distilling pineapple juice into alcohol on board the rig. He was a lot older than me and a real character. Norman 'Nock' Linton is deceased now, and the alcohol eventually had a lot to do with his demise.

There are many sayings about the oil industry and one of them used to be that you spend half your life trying to get into the industry and the other half trying to get out! That ended up being very true for a lot of people. It is an industry with people from all walks of life, from ex-forces and fishermen from North East of Scotland to waifs and strays from life - you can guess what category I fit into.

The list of jobs I had before getting into the oil industry is endless. I did not like nor really care about any of them and the expression more clubs than golfer Jack Nicholas or football manager Tommy Docherty, definitely fits with me. Work was just a means to have money (or beer tokens) for the weekend. What attracts people to the oil industry is not just the money, but also the time off. With being a relatively young industry, the prospects were there for you to end up with a lucrative and long-term career, doing a job that only you understand coming from within the industry.

My lucky break came in 1985. The good old UK government ran a four-week basic rig crew course in Montrose, Scotland. They even had a small land rig to teach you all the basics for getting a job with a drilling contractor. The first step was the local Job Centre to complete an application form and sit a basic exam to see if you had anything between your ears. Another Selkirk lad who I know very well unfortunately fell at this hurdle. The thing is, Malcolm 'Pedlar' Pringle was a grafter and he would have done well. When the letter finally arrived for me to make my way to Montrose, I was very keen to say the least. Off I went in my trusty old P registered Volvo. The miles I had already covered in this old tank were massive - all mainly with a 'Tax in the Post' note on the windscreen.

There were sixteen of us in the class of '86, and although I cannot remember all the guys' names, I did meet a few again over the years. Mark Jones is one I will never forget as we shared a room at the lodgings - a great guy, from the Port Talbot area. Never ever met Mark again but through email and other modern technology we still keep in touch from time to time. It was Mark who helped me big time because after we completed the four-week basic rig crew course it was made clear to me that the RGIT Survival certificate was also required or nobody would take me on. Mark knew I was skint at the time and helped me out financially to pay for this. If you are reading this Mark, a big thanks once again although I'm pretty sure I paid you back! We stayed on at the digs in Montrose and travelled back and forward to King Street in Aberdeen in the old green tank.

There was another lad, James 'Jas' Cockburn from Stirling. How can you forget anyone with a name like that? Jas had a

2

tremendous sense of humour (which is helpful in the oil industry) and was just back from Australia. We often talked about Australia as I did three trips to Oz between 1980 and 1983, and we actually knew the same pub in Manly, on the North shore of Sydney. The New Brighton Hotel was a great watering hole. Jas was with another Scots lad who apparently did not like swearing in the pub and would often chastise, in his broad Scots accent, 'Divee think it's oot side yir in'. As you can imagine these immortal words were used a lot on the four-week course and the English lads didn't have a clue what he, in fact any of us, were saying. As for the other guys I remember one lad from North Berwick who stayed in a camper van, a lad from Bishop Auckland (Jimmy) who I met many years later in Singapore and ended up with his family there as the materials man on new builds – a good job, for sure. There was also the big lad Williamson who I also met in later years in the Middle East. He was an Assistant Driller and an ex-forces guy who would have made it all the way with SAS but for an accident that caused lung problems. You should have seen this guy dive at the local swimming pool. There was one lad who really had a brass neck and made it as an Offshore Company Representative - a really good job and the wages to go with it, an ex JCB excavator owner-operator. You should have seen his face when I walked into his office years later! Hands up to all you guys.

After completing both courses looking for a job in Aberdeen was still a difficult task as the slump of '86 had just kicked in. I returned to Selkirk and back to meaningless jobs hoping that one day a letter would arrive. There was one silver lining though, as it was during this return that I met my wife of over 30 years. How Judith has put up with me over the years beats me. Being married only once in the oil industry is a very rare. We bought a wee flat in Selkirk and with Judith making a good salary as a civil servant and I working shifts in one of the local tweed mills we were not bad off. But it bugged me that Judith was making more money than me! That was about to change.

Chapter 2

Thistle Alpha Platform (Santa Fe)

I was really starting to think that all the training and money had been for nothing as the wait for word from the oil companies and drilling contractors continued. We were not married yet, but really enjoying setting up home and being with each other. It was a good time in both of our lives.

Selkirk is not the easiest place to come from when it comes to people trying to better themselves or indeed break free of the circle of dead-end jobs. I know this will be said about a lot of small rural towns but unfortunately Selkirk takes the biscuit here. My Grandfather Jimmy Doug used to often say, 'What a grand wee place Selkirk is, it's just a pity about some of the bastards that are in it'. I never thought much about his opinion, or maybe warning, until later in life when he was certainly proven to be right. I always liked to hear of people doing well, and knocking others down was something I never strived to do, but unfortunately there are a lot of people in Selkirk who thrive on casting gossip and malice. They are usually the ones who have never seen or done anything of significance themselves. Selkirk in my early days was a thriving small industrial town with busy tweed mills, but sadly these are all mostly gone now and the town is such an exciting place these days that even the salmon have stopped coming up the River Ettrick.

I will never forget the day at the mill when a colleague informed me that, 'Jimmy Doug, yir Grandfather's looking for yee'. Out I go to see the old fella standing waving a letter in front of me. It was from Santa Fe. I had used my Grandfather's address when looking for a job in Aberdeen. The interview was organised over the phone and off I went to Aberdeen again. This time only an interview and medical stood in my way. Steve Taylor was the personnel officer at Santa Fe and when he asked me when I could start, I couldn't hide my delight. It was a four-month trial as a trainee roustabout, on a two-weeks-on and two-weeks-off rota. The money was not the best but at least I was in the door. The

4

starting rate was £2.20 per hour for eight hours, then four hours at time-and-a-half, time-and-a-half on Saturdays and double time on Sundays. There was also an offshore bonus and a £75 retainer to ensure you returned back after your time off. If you made it through the trial there was a contract waiting with full wages.

I made my way by train from Edinburgh to Aberdeen on a March Monday in 1987 and headed straight to the Bon Accord Street guest house of Santa Fe, called Ferndale. It was run by dear old Mrs Howie. It was, at best, basic and stank of cats' piss. There were two, and sometimes three, guys to a room. All of them mostly 'three sheets to the wind', knowing that come the Tuesday morning there would be no more booze for 14 days. After a bit of breakfast, for those who were sober and hungry, I was picked up by minibus and taken to Bristow's helicopter base at Dyce, next to Aberdeen Airport. On Tuesday morning I was to make my first long chopper journey to Thistle Alpha. Waiting for me with the Santa Fe van driver were two pairs of coveralls – one for off-shift and one for on – a pair of safety boots, yellow steel-toe-capped wellingtons, thermals, a white safety helmet and a water-proof jacket. One thing I should add is that in 1987 there was no breathalyser before going offshore, or indeed any drug testing. There were guys being carried into the helicopter base, helped into their survival suit, or body bags as we called them, even being assisted to complete their boarding card details because they were too drunk to write.

When you approach an oil platform for the first time they can be fairly intimidating – a huge metal jungle comes to mind. Arriving in the heli-deck waiting room was a Santa Fe rep to take me to the office before being given a guided tour around the cabins, communal showers and toilets, mess room, boot locker room, cinema and the coffee shack for smoke breaks. A lot to take on-board would be the understatement of the year. How different things are these days with proper safety Inductions – there was no such thing then. I remember the Tool Pusher telling me, '…first time offshore? Keep yourself safe son, do your work and go home in one piece'. That was it.

The shift pattern was twelve hours on and twelve hours off, with a horrendous shift change in the middle. Shifts started at noon and finished at midnight for the first week. In the North Sea it takes four crews to run a rig. When I arrived one crew – a complete back to back crew – were leaving the rig for their fourteen days off to be replaced by the crew I was arriving with for our fourteen days. The other crew were at home starting their second week off. While the fourth crew were midway through the two weeks of their hitch, off-shore. The horrendous shift change is on final shift of week one, when you start work as normal at noon but finish at 6pm, only to return for a twelve-hour shift at midnight. The following day was one where you could practically sleep on your feet. Twelve-hour shifts take a bit of getting used to but when you add the short six-hour turnaround it was exhausting. The bonus was that on your final shift you finished at 6am – in time for the helicopter to take you back to shore, if it arrived. If there was no helicopter because of adverse weather conditions such as fog, then it was back to your cabin to change into work clothes to continue the shift until the replacement crew finally arrived. If your back to back did not arrive that day you would be requested to stay on board until a replacement was found. To refuse meant things would be made very difficult for you and chances of promotion would dissolve. I never experienced the treatment, but often saw it happen to others.

My first couple of shifts were with an experienced roustabout. I practically followed him everywhere. He was a Glasgow lad, if my memory serves me correctly, and I can remember him saying, 'you are here now pal – that is you a North Sea tiger'. Things have changed over the years but Santa Fe's approach to sending fresh-faced arrivals with an experienced roustabout was a good move. A few years after me becoming a North Sea tiger, it all changed with extensive safety inductions being introduced and green helmets provided for all new workers. I soon discovered why I'd been issued with thermals to wear beneath overalls. No matter what time of year it is, the North Sea is a hostile weather environment. We often used to laugh about seeing the four seasons in one day – although it mostly felt like winter. No matter what the weather was if casing (well liner) or drill pipe required moving on the deck you were out in it.

During those early days, my immediate boss was the crane operator, big Bezzy from York shire. He had been offshore for years and had me doing all sorts of jobs, such as painting, cleaning decks, moving pipe work about the deck, signalling the crane, slinging loads, and moving chemicals in the store. This was my chance and I was not going to let it pass me by. Santa Fe would not let you near the drill floor during the first trip, which was fair enough. They were also extremely strict on tea breaks, or 'smoko breaks' as they were called, and meal breaks. Platforms in the North Sea were bonded and there was a duty-free shop on board. Everyone seemed to smoke in those days and 200 Embassy Regal would cost around £6.50. Smoko breaks worked with four roustabouts taking it in turn – one at a time – taking fifteen minutes twice before meal break and twice after, with the meal-break lasting half an hour. It was important never to stay over your fifteen minutes for a smoko, as it would eat into the time the others had. It was the same with meal breaks. Now, try washing your hands, stripping off layers of clothes, making your way to the galley, queuing and then finally eating your meal – all in thirty minutes.

The food on the Thistle Platform was good. According to the crane operator, compared to what had been served up in the past it was rubbish. I'm pretty sure you would not eat like that at home. The timed smokos and meal-breaks was Santa Fe's way of keeping everything in check. To say I did not like this regimented way would be an understatement. I could understand this reasoning for rules if things were busy on the deck, but if things were quiet why treat people like this? Santa Fe was an old, traditional American drilling contractor and that was their way. I began to settle in and the practical jokes were rife.

'Can you go and get a bucket of steam?"'

'Have you seen the keys to the V door (V door is the huge entrance to drill floor)?'

'Go to the mechanics shop and get a left-handed hammer.'

I'm pleased to say I never fell for any of them. But later down the road I did see another new trainee Roustabout wandering about aimlessly with a bucket. The mind boggles. One thing I did like was when you went out on shift you never really knew what job you were going to be doing. The variety kept things interesting. One easy job was to be the firewatcher for the rig welder. All you did was stand with a fire extinguisher and 'bullshit' with the welder. In this case it was an old guy who must have worked all over the world with Santa Fe. Danny McWilliams was his name – an ex-shipyard Glaswegian – and you could listen to his stories all day. Coming to the end of his days offshore the Thistle Platform or 'Black Pig', as it was nicknamed, was perfect for Danny. On my second week I met Danny's son Eddie. He was the crane operator on the crew that had just come on board when we short-changed to second week. Everybody said then, and I remember it very well, that Eddie's crew was by far the best to work with. Little did I know then that we were going to bump into each other many times over the years and become good friends, as you will read in the forthcoming chapters.

With my first hitch coming to an end it was time for the helicopter 'to the beach'. First stop, pub or off licence for a carry-out to enjoy on the train to Edinburgh. If time allowed, we would do both. I've always been partial to a drink or two, and after fourteen days without any, you can imagine how that first beer tasted. The thing is with living in an offshore temperance hotel for fourteen days, the booze would go straight to your head. Judith used to pick me up at Waverley Railway Station in Edinburgh as there were no trains to the Borders in those days, and the coach journey was horrendous. Unfortunately, the offers of lifts did not last long after several warnings for arriving in Edinburgh the worse for wear. At least I never fell asleep on the train journey, as one guy did and finally woke up when the train was pulling into Doncaster. The taxi fare from Doncaster to Selkirk put him off drinking for a long time, I can assure you. Over the years I heard of many guys sleeping through to Berwick upon Tweed, but not as far as south Yorkshire.

If you live in the Aberdeen area your hitch is a symmetrical fourteen/fourteen, but if you were like me and many others from other parts of the UK it really is sixteen/twelve. Your last day on shore was travelling back to Aberdeen and your first day off the rig was travelling home. However, it is your choice of occupation and career. Where else could you get a job where for fourteen days all your meals are provided, your bed is made and changed for you, where home is walking distance from your place of work and all your washing done for you. The time off was great with good money in your pocket! The oil Industry was the first place where I heard of people talking about going on good holidays during their time off – that stuck with me. It was an enjoyable life that I'd found for myself, and now I just had to be fortunate that the ticking time bomb we lived on for fourteen days didn't go off.

The pubs in Selkirk at this time were usually busy places and you would often get greeted with enquiries of how you were getting on. One annoying question, within minutes of coming through the door, was when you'd be asked, 'aye you just back then? When do you go away again now?' This was often on my first day or two back. One thing I will say, the twelve days at home certainly went a lot quicker than the fourteen offshore.

Back on the rig and it was time for me to become 'justabout' a roustabout. To relieve the roughnecks for their smoke and meal breaks I was introduced to the drill floor. After only learning on a small land rig, the scale took me completely by surprise. They were a street-wise lot those roughnecks and this was one of the few times that I was caught out with a practical joke. The experienced floor men would stick paper cups on your helmet with drill pipe dope, the lubricant for thread joints. It became a competition to see how many cups they could stick to my helmet without me noticing – I think my count was four or five. Not as bad as one of the boys who had seven. I can't remember a lot of the guys' names but the derrick man was Eddie McCarl from Clydebank. Another roughneck was from Perth, Jock Burrell, and there was also Chalky from Rhodesia. Everything according to Chalky everything was 'fucking pish'. Despite the practical jokes they were all good lads. Eddie had me up the derrick one shift and asked me if I felt confident enough to pull in a string of drill pipe. You have a safety belt on and you lean out of the monkey board to throw a rope round the pipe and release the elevators. You then pull the ninety feet of drill pipe back into the rack. I was game but the driller stopped us in our tracks, as he was having none of it. Looking back, I cannot blame him, as if I had messed up it would have been him and the derrickman who would have had to face the music.

I remember one night on the deck we were bringing casing, which is steel liner for the well, on board. I still don't know what

9

happened at the landing area but I'm glad I had my wits about me as the steel bundle, weighing approximately five tonnes, came crashing down from about twelve feet above onto the deck. The crane operator came rushing down to enquire if I was okay. 'I don't know what happened there wee man come up to crane', he said. What he did not know, was that years ago when I was young, I used to spend time with an old 19 Ruston Bucyrus crane operator, and I had a good idea how everything worked. He went over the joystick controls and asked me if I wanted to have a play. The boom is huge on one of these and you have a lot of rope compared to an old 19 RB, but the basics are the same. Little did I know but this was going to serve me well in years to come.

One of the more common jobs during those early days was to wash and clean the mud pits. These days you require a confined space training certificate as well as a specific work permit. There is also a requirement now for at least three workers to be present. Not then. You were handed a shovel, hose, and rubber squeegee on the end of a brush shank and off you went on your own until someone relieved you for a smoke break. The smell of the chemicals and whatever gases had emerged from the bowels of the earth were in the old mud. When I think about those times now it was stupidity, but you were ignorant to the danger. With confined space accidents there are not many people who live to tell the tale. Years later when studying safety, confined space entry was still fresh in my memory and it horrified me on the cleaning procedures we adopted on the Black Pig.

My four month trial period was over and I became a fully-fledged and fully paid roustabout. It worked out at an extra couple of hundred pounds for each trip. It was certainly more than I could ever have earned in the mills in Selkirk. When you consider you were living cash free for half the month the money seemed all the more. I continued doing my roughneck-relieving when required. One thing which sticks in my mind from that time was the continual shouting and bawling when on the drill floor. There were times when nobody knew what the hell was going on! There were no pre-shift meetings or ongoing toolbox meetings to discuss what was happening. I don't think the driller liked himself never mind the people around him. George McNeill was a tough guy – the rigs' version of Irvine Welsh's

Francis Begbie character. He was violent man, some would say verging on being a psychopath. He was smallish in stature but strong in the right places and had earned the nickname La Motta after the Raging Bull boxer Jake La Motta. I remember one night there was another roustabout called Odd Job. Bald heads were rare then and this guy must have looked old when he was a teenager; public school educated and not a bad bloke. Anyway, he was painting near the drill floor and La Motto walked past him and told him he had missed a bit. La Motto grabbed the paint roller out of his hand and reached to try and paint the area, but unfortunately being small he couldn't reach. Odd Job remarked about him being too short and McNeill responded by taking the roller and ramming it into his mouth before walking away.

After your twelve hours, it was time to shower, change into your fresh coveralls, grab some ice cream and then off to the cinema for a movie and enjoy some banter before bed. There was always plenty of laughs to keep spirits high. This communal-type gathering doesn't happen now as almost all rigs have televisions in the cabins, and with computers and internet access off-shifts can be fairly solitary. In 1987 there was none of this. You relied on newspapers coming out by helicopter, letters from home and the occasional telephone call to find out what was happening at home.

Nearing the end of one hitch it was agreed by all to meet at a bar called Platform 9 in Aberdeen for a drink before heading down the road. Most of the guys were there including McNeill. While joking around Eddie McCarl threw his arms around a seated La Motto from behind. Now as you know it is almost impossible to get out of the chair when someone has you pinned from behind. McNeill huffed and puffed and put up a hell of a struggle to get out of the chair and in the end both he and Eddie were on the floor. I was in the toilet when McNeill walked in and looked at the mirror. He had the slightest graze or small scratch on the bridge of his nose. Well, he went absolutely berserk, ran back out to everyone sitting nervously enjoying a drink, shouting 'right I am marked (pointing at his nose) the whole lot of you outside am taking the fucking lot of you on'. Another roustabout I got on with well was Allan Ridley from the Gateshead area. We nodded at each other and were off like two sprinters coming out

11

of the blocks. We were certainly not hanging around there with 'Begbie' on the rampage. I grabbed a couple of beers for the train and settled down for the journey. We agreed to 'never doing that again for sure'. A few miles into the journey, and who the hell appears coming down the carriage. Looking like a man possessed, McNeill! He threw us a dirty look, shouting 'fucking pair of poofs' and stormed off down the train. Lucky to say, we never saw him again before Edinburgh Waverley.

On our next trip the Platform 9 incident was never mentioned, so things returned to normal. I had a few things in common with McNeil - we were both Hibs supporters and had an interest in boxing. He apparently was a good boxer but obviously never made it professionally. He once asked me about some of the boxers from Selkirk, there were a few good ones in the years previously, especially Bobby Black. I'd sparred with Bobby as a young guy and enjoyed the sport but only as a junior. Bobby was middle weight champion of Scotland for years and McNeil said he had heard of him. Bobby was once flown down to London to spar with a middle weight called Mark Naylor who was having a tilt at a world title and needed a good sparring partner as there were none in his area fitting the bill. Bobby had once defeated this guy in an amateur fight, but after Naylor improved it was one-way traffic and Bobby never beat him again. McNeill told me if you ever fancy a couple of rounds in the chemical store give me a shout! Eh, no thanks. To this day I hope he was joking!

On a night out in Edinburgh with Jock Burrell, he phoned McNeill to come and meet us for a drink. Although my wife and I nervously tagged along, old La Motta turned out to be brilliant company. When we walked into one bar, though, you could see the respect this guy received from the regulars. It was a bit like the old westerns, walking into a saloon with a gun slinger and the respect that greeted him. McNeill was obviously very well known as a tough guy.

The Thistle Alpha has twin derrick towers. In 1987 one was used for all work overs and any drilling work. The other was never used but Santa Fe had a couple of guys there all the time doing basic maintenance work should the derrick and drilling unit ever be required. Because of the maintenance it would be operational in no time. During one shift the crane operator sent me up to the unused derrick tower to collect a couple of things and when I arrived at the drill floor I heard someone whistling and singing. Here was one of the maintenance guys standing with a daft grin on his face. The more I looked, I realised this guy was rather inebriated. 'How the hell did you get into this state', I enquired? 'Easy', was the reply and he pulled an orange out of his jacket pocket. What this character was doing was injecting oranges with vodka and bringing them offshore. He even told me how he was stopped once and asked why he was taking oranges offshore as there were plenty offshore already?

'Aye', he responded, 'but there aren't any Outspan Oranges'. It turned out that the Outspan sticker acted as a cover for the needle marks.

On the Thistle, I was part of the drill crew. There was another company called Lassalle, responsible for all the helicopter landings and refuelling as well as other deck lifts not concerning drilling. They had an easy job compared to what we had to put up with. It was nearing the end of a hitch one day when one of their guys in the coffee shop told me that he heard that there was a company called Dyvi Offshore in Norway looking for roughnecks but you had to have the Montrose certificate to get a job with them in the Norwegian sector of the North Sea. It was two weeks on, three weeks off, followed by two weeks on and then four weeks off according to the Lassalle guy. Apparently, it was good money as well. I had completely forgotten about Dyvi Offshore until my last day at home.

Chapter 3

Offshore Norway, Dyvi Stena

By this point I had been with Santa Fe for around eight or nine months and could roughneck. I could proudly call myself an experienced North Sea tiger. However the oil slump was still going on and promotion opportunities were rare with everybody just glad to have a job. I would be telling fibs to say that I was over the moon with Santa Fe, especially all the shouting and roaring on the drill floor, as well as the sixteen-twelve rotation. Judith and I were out for a walk on the final day of home leave - a Monday to make matters worse - and we were both feeling rather low, another two weeks away again! Then out of the blue I remembered about what I'd been told about the job in Norway. As we were walking past a phone box across from the old Templeton's supermarket in Selkirk I quickly explained to Judith about what I had heard, and said, 'Why don't I try this?'

'Up to you', was the reply. I telephoned directory enquiries for the number of Dyvi Offshore in Aberdeen and quickly made the call. 'No jobs here', was the answer from the girl on other end of the phone 'Why don't you phone Stavanger office on transfer charges, if they are looking for personnel they will possibly accept.' She kindly provided the number and I phoned the operator to see if they would accept the call. To my surprise they accepted, and their first question was, 'do you have your Montrose certificate?'. When I replied that I did, I was then asked if I had a survival certificate and who I was working with. When I revealed that I did have a survival certificate and I was with Santa Fe, they came back with 'when can you start?' It was true about the shift patterns. They told me the rotation would be two weeks on and three weeks off, then two weeks on and four weeks off. When he told me the wages would be in Norwegian Kroner, my first reply was that is okay for the two weeks on but what about the three weeks and four weeks off? The money would be for a monthly salary. I could not believe my ears! The Norwegian continued, 'if you want the job you will need to travel to

Aberdeen tomorrow for medical and bring your certificates, on completion of medical, hotel overnight in Aberdeen and then fly to Stavanger. We shall organise a helicopter seat to the rig, where you will join your crew'. I held my hand over the phone and explained the scenario to Judith. Neither of us could believe what was happening. 'Okay', was my next (would have been a fool not to take the job) remark, 'I will take the job'. I gave the Dyvi personnel guy my home telephone number and that was that.

After an excited walk home, the lady from Dyvi Offshore in Aberdeen phoned to provide their office address and make arrangements for a medical on the Tuesday afternoon and also remind me to bring all of my paperwork along.

'Where is your nearest airport'" she asked. 'Edinburgh' was my reply. 'Do you need a flight for tomorrow, or can you catch a train and we will reimburse your train ticket cost when you arrive in Aberdeen?' I could not believe my ears. I thought about phoning Santa Fe to inform them I was not returning, but felt it would be safer to wait until after my medical. I would be in deep trouble anyway for missing a crew change. I made my way to Aberdeen the next day and arrived at Dyvi Offshore's little office. I passed the medical, then the lady in the office booked me into a good hotel for the night.

'The crew you will likely be joining shall have ten-to-eleven days to do then I'm not sure if you are off for three or four weeks. You will find this out on the rig'.

She then handed me a flight ticket to Stavanger, my train ticket money and £100 expenses in case of any extras. Was this really happening?

'Oh, and here is an expenses sheet that goes with your time sheet, do not put any more expenses in for this month as I have just given you £100!'

I made my way to the hotel and decided to enjoy a few beers while I digested everything. One minute I was being treated like a piece of shit on board the Thistle platform, and now I was being given a taste of the good life. I phoned Santa Fe to inform them that I was not coming back. When the rig manager of Thistle phoned back, I was really surprised by his comment. Instead of the expected 'never phone us again', he said, 'sorry you are going but that is life and if things do not work out get in touch and if there is a vacancy the job will be yours'. Looking back, I'm glad I never closed the door with Santa Fe as our paths were going to cross again a good few years later when starting my own business.

I flew to Stavanger following a very relaxing night in a cracking hotel in Aberdeen. The heliport in those days was at the airport. It wasn't long after that Norway had its own purpose-built heliport servicing all the oil industry offshore from Stavanger. I eventually flew out to the Dyvi Stena to start another adventure. After a brief induction, I met the other guys on board. The atmosphere I noted straight away was much better than that on the Thistle Platform. Yet again, though, I felt like a fish out of water. The semi-submersible drilling rig was certainly a lot different to a Platform. Being a floater, the movement was a shock, for a start. The accommodation cabins, with their own shower and bathroom, was another novelty. There was also the sleeping rota - one week on top bunk and second week on bottom bunk. I started my shift and, without sounding too technical, was amazed by all the automatic devices the Dyvi Stena had. There was no shouting or screaming here. It did not take me long to fit in, even although I was a novice on a drilling rig. You could tell, though, that the experienced drill crew were not sure why UK guys were on board taking Norwegian jobs. I never thought about that at the time with being a newcomer but was soon to realise further down the road that most Norwegians did not want a job on a drilling rig - they wanted an easier time on a platform. It was a good bit later during my time in Norway that I landed on a platform. I can assure you these platforms in Norway are like five-star hotels! It was no wonder the locals wanted a job on a platform.

The company's personal protective equipment such as safety boots and coveralls was much better than the North Sea sector. The only thing that was not as good was the 'Jallatte' rigger boots - I always liked these better than Red Wings, as they were too heavy. I wonder if they are still as good these days.

Smoke breaks and meal breaks were much more relaxed in Norway as well. When things were quiet on the rig floor, the driller would send two roughnecks away for meal break and, as long as you did not take too long, nothing was said. As for smoke breaks, you were more or less left to sort yourselves out. As long as you were ready to put the shift in when required nobody bothered you. When I finished my first hitch I was informed that I'd now be off for four weeks. I headed home excited and when my first salary hit the bank we both thought we had won the Littlewoods football coupon! The only thing about this four weeks off was that when returning to the rig it was going to be my first Christmas and New Year offshore. I just had to get on with it. The food on board at Christmas and New Year was something else. The Norwegians have their main Christmas Dinner on Christmas Eve, and to make us feel at home they did another one on the 25th as well! Auld Year's Night, or Hogmanay as we call it in Scotland, was strange being offshore, but we knew we were soon going to end our hitch and it would be three weeks off this time. I cannot remember exactly what happened nearing crew change but word soon got round that we were going to fly home in a chartered flight, not a scheduled flight. Following the crew change helicopter into Stavanger we were met by the lady from the Aberdeen office who had come across for a meeting. She travelled across in the chartered flight - there was ten maybe twelve of us heading home with smiles on our faces like Cheshire cats.

I'll never forget when we boarded the chartered plane and she opened up a couple of boxes full to the brim with booze - Happy New Year boys! You can guess the rest! Judith was not very pleased at what eventually arrived in Edinburgh but when the salary dropped into my account for being offshore at Christmas and New Year, it was smiles all round.

Things changed dramatically on the next trip. We were all summonsed to the recreation room to be informed that Dyvi Offshore had been sold to Smedvig. But the Dyvi Stena was not part of the sale and we were all now working for a new company called Seatec Offshore, founded by the higher management within Dyvi Offshore. Ernie Lawrence, or Sizzler as he was nick named, was the Offshore Installation Manager and had the most horrendous lisp. He called the company Theetec! If you want to keep your job you will "Thign on for Theetec or leave the rig and join Thmedvig". Anyone familiar with Monty Python would have felt like they were thrown into the Life of Brian with Woger.

Obviously none of us UK guys left the rig but I do think a few Norwegians decided to move on. As if this was not bad enough, things were going to get a lot worse! We were coming out of the hole just about to put the Kelly on (a device then used for pumping mud down the well) when BANG, CRASH, it hit the bushings on the rig floor. The driller and tool pusher came running out of the drillers shack and shouted, 'Underground explosion! Get the fuck off the drill floor!'

Now I had no idea what this was, but when it was explained to me we had been very, very lucky not to get blown out of the water. Apparently at the bottom of the well there had been different pressures and this had caused an explosion. Luckily for us it had not travelled (yet) up the (annulus) to the top of the well. But we were in a very precarious position because if it did travel up the well it would have meant abandoning the rig immediately.

It took a further nine to ten worrying months before the Dyvi Stena, with another rig having to drill relief wells, was finally able to raise the Blow Out Preventers (BOPs) and head for a shipyard to be fully overhauled. This was going to take a good while so unfortunately a skeleton crew was all that was required and the rest of us were laid off until the rig was going back out to work. I picked up a job on the Ocean Odyssey, and this was the same time as the Piper Alpha disaster. We were actually not too far away from where this terrible accident happened.

Judith and I decided to get married around this time and with this in mind and a honeymoon to look forward to I decided, that the UK sector of the North Sea was definitely not for me and quit the job onboard Ocean Odyssey. You can well imagine my disbelief when reading the news a week later that the Ocean Odyssey, within weeks of the Piper Alpha, had also taken a massive kick (blow out) and was on fire! There was only one fatality. A radio operator who did not know the rig with being a new start was sent back from the lifeboat to the radio room to send out another SOS, and was never heard of again. Poor guy! The tool pusher who sent him back was never brought to court in the UK for his actions. Somehow clever expensive lawyers managed to ensure there was no extradition order.

18

With wedding celebrations and the honeymoon all but a distant memory it was a sigh of relief to receive the phone call from Norway to inform me the Dyvi Stena had secured further contracts, and so it was back to Norway for me to join the crew. I'm pleased to say there were no more underground explosions and the rig drilled many wells offshore. Yes, there were a few problems along the way, as there always is when drilling an exploration well, but nothing like the tragedies that had happened around that time. Our crew changes out of other areas in Norway, including Kristiansand in the north. What a beautiful place, and of course Bergen too. This was when the penny finally dropped that a lot of Scots words come from the old Norwegian languages. The Viking days naturally would have led to this - hospital in Norwegian is 'syc hoose', while a 'barn' in Norse is a child, similar to our bairn in Scots. One of the funniest of them all has to be a vacuum cleaner in Norse being a 'stoor sooker'!

On the recommendation of the Norwegians, I decided to join the union and this turned out to save me from being dismissed! We had this shocking old American company man from Louisiana who was very perturbed about this two on three off, and two on four off rotation we were working. He was very vocal about this. On one occasion he had a few trainee drilling engineers on the drill floor and started to show them how to use rig tongs and other hand tools. Why he was allowed to do this beats me, but these guys do think they are tin gods! Anyway one of the wires holding the rig tong managed to get caught on a bull dog grip and instead of the old fool stopping and taking a look up, he shouted and roared at these bewildered trainee engineers to push and push obviously going nowhere. Instead of shutting my mouth I whistled, pointed up at the wire caught on the bulldog and let out a laugh. He went absolutely berserk. Next thing I knew I was in OIM's office, Sizzler (again), being threatened with the sack. Or as it was put to me you could still join Thmedvig in the UK 'thector'. No way! Looks as though you will be 'thacked' then! I carefully pulled out my union card and the look on Sizzlers face said it all.

'Better get the union rep in here' I replied.

To cut a long story short, to end the ridiculous situation I was demoted to roustabout for a few trips until things quietened down. I joined the crane operator's crew on the next shift and there was little difference in money. It was certainly much easier than roughnecking – and with over time I ended up better off! I kept my mouth shut from there on and just popped away, keeping well away from the old red neck when he was onboard. It wasn't long before I started to get more and more interested in learning to operate these offshore cranes on board the Dyvi Stena. The cranes were manufactured by Liebherr from Austria, state of the art, with prices to match. After having a good talk with one operator of the electric hydraulic pedestal marine crane, I started with just getting used to the length and size of the boom and of course controlling the hook. My crane operator, Peter Armstrong was a good lad, old school, but he certainly put me in the correct direction. I learned a lot from Peter, but he always warned me to beware of the dreaded OIM Sizzler as he was out for me apparently at the first chance he could get, because of the rig floor and union card scenario. This proved true. One night at around three in the morning, fast asleep in my bunk I was summonsed to OIM's office immediately. Apparently someone had lifted a load over a wire line that was feeding a service company's tool down the well. This is a big NO on a drilling rig because if anything happened to the wire line it could cost millions in damages with trying to retrieve from down the well.

After being questioned about myself being in the crane, I had no idea what I was being accused of. Later that morning one of the Norwegian roughnecks held up his hand and admitted to moving a load of some kind over the wire line. No apology to me and nothing apparently ever said to the roughneck, as far as I was aware. I maybe should have pulled the union card again but decided not to.

One of the heaviest and most awkward lifts on the rig was the riser joint from the drill floor, where there was a special landing area and the need for special slings to lift it level. Peter provided instructions and allowed me to carry out this lift on numerous occasions, because as with anything, the more you did it, the more competent you became. On this occasion one of the Norwegian roustabouts, a smashing fellow called Helge Tosse who taught me Norwegian by using children's comics, was on the tag lines controlling the load and he kept nodding his head. I was not sure why he kept nodding until the load was lowered properly into its place. When climbing down the crane Helge was there to inform me that the OIM, Sizzler, had been standing under the pedestal of the crane, just watching and hoping I would make a mess of the lift. Fortunately for me, I never. His turn was about to come regarding me though.

Peter was ill one day and I was left on my own on the deck in horrendous weather conditions. There was an urgent lift of steel casing from a supply vessel and I was asked to lift this onto the rig. Instead of saying 'NO', I informed them that I was out of my depth here but would have a try. What a mess I made of this lift. That is the only way I can describe it. I did not damage anything or hurt anyone but it was bloody awful. I ame very close to wiping the supply vessel's bridge out for sure, and even the captain said it was the worst operating he had seen since Bombay Heights! It also played right into Sizzler's hands, and the outcome was that I was banned from operating any of the 'cranth'.

My luck changed dramatically when Sizzler was moved on to a different rotation and our paths did not cross for many years.

Peter must have spoken with the new powers that be, because once I spoke with the OIM, Ron Sturridge, I was able to let him know that I was still keen to learn. I even offered to give up my meal break for a while if I could have the stand-by vessel come along beside the rig to practise various lifts. I mastered this surprisingly quickly and decided that during my next time at home to get my official stage 2 offshore crane operators' certificate at Sparrow's training centre near Aberdeen. I paid for this myself.

The five-day course at Aberdeen was quite good and coming from a drilling rig I enjoyed it. If I thought I made a mess of the lift in Norway what I was about to witness here was certainly in the same league, if not worse. The crane services company Sparrows had an old offshore crane set up next to a quarry and this was used along with various other cranes - crawler and mobile - for the course. An assistant crane operator from another drilling contractor was moving a container on a practical exercise when instead of picking up the container to a safe height slewed the crane round and wiped out the top of a tree next to main entrance which was next to an electric power station. With this being a five-day stage 2 course, I expected it to be curtains for this trainee but surprisingly nothing was really said! One of the other operators from the same company then told us that this assistant was on his last legs as an assistant as he had caused havoc on the rig he worked on. Apparently he lost control of the header ball one day and some of the other guys were in the galley talking about the poor operating on the deck when the header ball came smashing in through a port hole window landing on a table in the galley. The operator then, instead of stopping everything, realised what he had done and simply pulled on the hoist lever and the header ball disappeared back out the port hole. Funny in retrospect, but also dangerous. It could only happen in the oil industry!

When I got back to the rig with my new certificate, I was really pleased to be allowed to conduct lifts. We had a night captain at this time called Jimmy Wallace. What a character the old fisherman was. He knew the job well enough but, apparently, his qualifications were all forged and Jimmy just disappeared the same as he had appeared on the rig. I've come across a lot of great storytellers on the rig, but the stories he could tell took the biscuit. One night we were all sitting having a cup of tea in the coffee shop when enters the bold Jimmy, 'Eh, what a job getting home last trip', he tells us.

There we were sitting on the SAS flight to Aberdeen when one of the air hostesses made an announcement over the tannoy system for a Mr Jimmy Wallace to make himself known to the crew – 'the captain would like to speak with you in the cockpit, Jimmy', he continued.

'Hi Jimmy', said the captain, 'I wonder if you can assist here as we are lost in the fog and cannot find Aberdeen. Just take the plane down so I can see the sea and hopefully I will get my bearings'.

Once the Captain had taken the plane down Jimmy, apparently, let out a roar.

'There you are son that is Rattery Heights, well-known to fishermen. Just take the plane to the left and we will be over Peterhead then down to Aberdeen airport.'

By now Jimmy was in full flow and the entire coffee shop was listening. The hostess put it over the tannoy thanking Jimmy Wallace and everyone gave me a big round of applause. 'Can we offer you a drink Jimmy?' asks the hostess, 'Get everyone a drink,' came his reply.

Poor Alex Reid, the Sub Sea Engineer had to sit in front of Jimmy and listen to this and just more or less nod. Jimmy then finishes by looking at him, 'hell of a carry on Alex, eh?'

Enjoying a good laugh, myself, I knew that Jimmy's stories could be useful when working with him. One night when coming down from the crane Jimmy was standing looking out to sea and I just knew something was brewing on the story front.

'All right Jimmy?' I enquired.

'Aye, nae bother pal', came the reply.

'You look deep in thought' I said.

'I'm thinking of packing this offshore work in. I've just received a phone call from the Henry Ford car company in the States. Did you know I have a couple off garages on shore? They want me to take over the dealership in North of Scotland of the new Ford Granada!'

On another occasion, the bold Jimmy revealed the origins of a sword he owned.

'Just had that wife of mine on the phone and she wants to change the fireplace' he began.

'I've told her "don't you dare touch my sword on the top of the fireplace"'.

He continued, 'This sword is special to me - it was presented to me by the Emir of Oman when I saved the rig from rebel tribesmen. I was working offshore in Oman when the attack happened and as we were on a jack-up drilling rig when the rebel tribesmen tried to climb the legs, I ordered the crew to throw nuts and bolts, and pour buckets of oil over the top of them.'

Proudly smiling in reflection, he continued, 'Once we had repelled the attack and when the crew change came along, the Emir was there to thank me and presented me with this beautiful Arabic sword with a huge gemstone in centre of the handle. It has been on the fireplace ever since.'

Going on shift with Jimmy was a bit like 'Jackanory' story time.

We had a Norwegian welder who could tell a few long stories. His big one was that when on his time off he did secret work for NASA in the States welding rocket launchers. He was, apparently, not allowed to discuss this work but stated that he once broke his leg and was so important to NASA that they flew him to the States where he welded part of the rocket launcher from his wheelchair.

Maybe it was something in the drinking water with these guys, but it certainly entertained the rest of us.

I had enjoyed Norwegian hospitality up to this point. But following another successful drilling operation we were sent to the Rosenberg Shipyard for routine maintenance work. This was to be my first real taste of how expensive the country could be. I was on board again for Christmas, only this time I would be heading home the day after Boxing Day. Norwegian Merchant Navy rules state that when a vessel comes into a shipyard, a proper gangway must be installed to allow for the crew to leave the vessel when finishing their shift, and that there should be a float of cash for them to borrow from their wages. The first night in town… well, you can imagine what went on. Some of the Norwegian guys went AWOL as soon as the gangway and float were in place. The UK members of crew were a little apprehensive because of the price of drinks – even then it was well over £5 a pint. The local beer, called Towe, also gave you a very nasty headache. We used to joke it was made from old rope, as even after a few pints the stinking headache would arrive. A famous bar in Stavanger in those days was the 'Taket Roof' (Thatched Roof). I remember leaving there and it still sticks in my mind now that the taxi back to the shipyard and a slice of pizza cost me £35 - it was only a matter of 500 yards or so from the bar.

Arriving back to the rig that night, I have never seen so many intoxicated people lying all over the place. The Norwegians were worse than us Scots when they got started. Many of them could not even find their cabins and slept in the corridors.

One of the Norwegian roustabouts I worked with then never left the rig. If I had been gambling, I would have put my wages on Sven Petersen being the first down the gangway. But no, as he then informed us that years ago when he was a teenager his parents bought a new house and when he and a friend explored the property they found a still for making alcohol in the cellar. Apparently, this is common in Norway due to the high price of alcohol. Anyway, they also found a few bottles of ready-made moonshine and decided to give it a try. His friend never regained consciousness and Sven landed up in the syc hoose (hospital) for two weeks completely blind. Obviously after some time his sight came back but with losing a friend and almost his own life, he never drank again! It made me wonder if this is where the saying 'blind drunk' originates.

The company decided as it was Christmas and we were in the shipyard they would provide beer for our festive dinner. I brought aboard the container with the good stuff inside and when landing it next to the galley, I have never seen as many people attack a container. Goodness knows how many crates of beer went AWOL but after the OIM made an announcement most of the crates reappeared. The threat was that if the missing crates were not returned the lot would be sent back. It was a great experience in the shipyard but drinking and then operating an offshore crane early the next morning, especially a personnel basket, is not recommended. What happens in the shipyard is that usually everyone works six-to-six and there is only a few on night shift. Having a few beers until about midnight then back up for a 6am start catches you up very quickly.

After New Year and my time off it was back to the rig and we were all made aware that Seatec were taking over the management of another drilling rig called Treasure Hunter. A few of the guys transferred to that rig, but I'm pleased to say I never did, and when the stories came back about the state of the rig I was very pleased to have stayed clear.

Not long after this Seatec then brought a huge Russian Jack Up into Norwegian waters. They were so keen to bring this into Norwegian waters they almost lost it in heavy seas as it came close to running aground. The Norwegian Coastguard was not too happy as they had been told not to attempt the tow until the weather subsided. Someone in higher management though gave the call to go ahead and it was only a matter of 50 yards or so from running aground on a very rocky shoreline. It was very close to a disaster.

Training courses were very good around this time, and I remember attending a Fast Boat Rescue Pilot course in Stonehaven, just south of Aberdeen, a Basic Firefighting course in Chorley with Lancashire Fire Brigade, and the Banksman/Slinger course conducted on the rig. I was also sent to Aberdeen for my Helicopter Landing Officer training. This was the one that I really needed and wanted, to go with my Stage 2 Offshore Crane Operators certificate.

Gavin Smith was an ex Merchant seaman who I did a bit of work with as an assistant crane operator. The rig we were on had a new hydraulic top drive system and it constantly leaked hydraulic oil all over the helicopter landing deck. We were constantly mopping up spillage until one day it was decided to remove the netting, scrub the helideck and paint it. Once it was all completed, big Gavin and I were there to land the first helicopter after the refurbishment. When the helicopter approaches the rig it will first request to the radio room onboard the rig for clearance and then finally to the helicopter landing officer. The pilot will then provide the chopper call sign and simply ask if deck is clear for landing. Now Gavin likes a laugh and when the pilot asked if the deck was clear for landing, I could not believe my ears when he replied, 'clear for landing? It's fucking spotless'. I burst out laughing, but this shortly turned very sour as the pilot shut the helicopter down on landing and wanted Gavin sacked. He managed to talk his way out of the situation by stating it must have been someone else on the channel and not him. It was a lesson learned - no more wise cracks with pilots.

When you go on training courses with a Norwegian employer, the transport provided to get you to and from the venue was first class. The accommodation was every bit as good, and the extra money in your wages was an added bonus. These were perks for attending training courses and getting better qualifications - oil industry qualifications are valuable to have under your belt.

One of the Aberdeen guys, an assistant driller called John Norman, was speaking with me one day and told me about going out with various agencies on your time off for seven or so shifts.

Four weeks off during the winter in Scotland can be a long pull and I thought, 'well why not'. As John said, 'If you do not like it, just quit'. I spoke with a few agencies and ended up doing a few weeks here and there. It was great beer money on top of the regular salary, and for me, although unaware at the time, I was learning even more about offshore cranes. Each agency job took you out to a rig, where you were given an introduction and then left to familiarise yourself with a completely different machine compared to the Liebherr cranes on board Dyvi Stena. My first agency trip was on board the Ninian Central, as stand-by crane operator for seven days. The cranes were very old UK-manufactured Stothert and Pitt ones. They were large cranes compared to what I operated on the Dyvi Stena. What I noticed and learned here is that you are a long way from the platform to a supply vessel, and offloading and back loading to the vessels was tricky with so much rope spooling from the drum, but all in all it was a great experience. The agency work was also very relaxed, and I enjoyed both the experience and the extra cash.

On one occasion the agency sent me to an old semi called The Sinbad, with a Norwegian crane called a Bradvag on one side, and an American Manitowoc crawler crane, which had been converted to fit onto a pedestal, on the other. It was definitely not a marine crane and not the safest type to have onboard a drilling rig, as it can be very difficult to operate. Your hands and feet have to be continually moving the entire time to ensure the smooth operating of the crane. But what an experience this was - no diesel hydraulics here, this was simply an old mechanical crawler crane and it was clutches in and clutches out when you were on the controls. It was also very fast, perhaps too fast for an offshore operation, except when conducting supply vessel assignments. The fully experienced operator showed me round and to state I was nervous would have been an understatement, but as the operator informed me, 'if you can operate one of these you will operate any crane', and he was one-hundred percent correct. I started by writing little notes in a book and did simple lifts around the deck in an effort to get to know and master this old crane. After the seven shifts I was asked if I wanted a full-time job – no thanks, and off I went. The Sinbad was in UK waters but was crewed almost entirely by Irish crew. Now you try and go to Irish waters and get a job offshore with a UK passport, no chance.

Another agency trip I did around this time was on board a Houlder Marine drilling rig. The personnel onboard were all mainly from the North East of Scotland and had been there since day one. The cranes were National OS435, and believe it or not there are still rigs today who have these cranes on board - that is how good these are – and I really enjoyed my week there.

Finally, one little job that I did was on a dive support vessel offshore Humberside. I received the quickest induction to a crane that I have ever had. It was no wonder the other operator wanted away. Once in the crane, that was you there for the entire twelve hours! Meals were brought to the cabin. You were not allowed to leave the crane. The divers had a giant vacuum/blower that was attached to the crane and they were blowing sand away from a pipeline. Instead of this job being interesting as an operator, it was simply awful. You had no idea what was going on under the water and had to go by what I was told to do by the divers on the radio. To make matters worse you had to repeat every order given to you to ensure no mistakes. If a current caught hold of the cleaner the divers expected you to try and control it, now how can you control something that you cannot see? Pick up ten feet and stop! Swing to your left five feet and stop! You practically went to bed with these orders ringing in your head. I was over the moon when after four shifts the company had hired a full-time operator and as I was free to go. They did not have to ask me twice.

Back on the Dyvi Stena I was informed we were going to be changing our coveralls again as Stena Drilling were now the new owners of the rig. Seatec Offshore were finally finished. Nothing really changed, except we now had a different employer. What I did not fully realise during this time was the experience I was gaining by going to other rigs and this was about to start serving me very well..

I received a message to contact main office as there was a General Safety course going to be conducted in Oslo and my name was on the list. I tried my best to dodge this course, but I'm glad I never as this opened my eyes. My attempted excuse was that I had to look after four roustabouts, the two cranes and all the HLO work. During this time the standard of local roustabouts that Stena Drilling were sending to the rig was shocking. They had no experience and didn't really want to learn - meaning we were left, when things were busy, running around doing everything. The office informed me that since I was in the crane, and could see everything going on, it was for me to stop any unsafe act immediately and I should be on the course. Without really knowing it then, this was one of the best training courses I ever attended, and I identified an opening to become more and more involved with safety.

The Norwegian sector was, and still is, the best in the world to work for. It was at this time that Judith was two weeks late with the birth of our first born. There were complications and Amy was born in August 1990 by emergency caesarean section. She was taken into intensive care afterwards - it was a very worrying time. I phoned the office and explained everything that had happened and also ask if I could have another week off work. 'No problem Craig, join the crew (Big Gavin's crew) that will come out the following week and we will take it from there', came the reply. I was pleased to say everything settled down and both mother and daughter recovered well. I joined Gavin's crew as his assistant for a week. Gavin was promoted from assistant crane operator to crane operator. His crane operator, an old Danish guy who had been in the oil industry for ever and a day, had recently married a girl a fraction of his age and life offshore started to get to him. They often found him in tears in the coffee shop, wishing he could finish working offshore altogether. This was taken out of his hands not long after, when he appeared at the helicopter base in Stavanger drunk as a lord armed with a carry out to take offshore. It was game over for him!

I remember a crew change around this time that had a hint of humour about it. The rig mechanic, who we nicknamed the Rig Pig, was Alex McCulloch. He was originally from Glasgow and now living up North, around the Nairn area. Alex was a character and we always knew when spare-ribs were on the menu at lunch time as Alex could not wait to go round the rig with barbecue sauce all over his mouth telling everyone how good the ribs were. Now, Alex liked a drink and it did not matter about cost on a crew change. All Alex wanted after fourteen days offshore was to get as drunk as he possibly could. I also remember meeting him when he first came back offshore. As you can imagine, some of his hangovers after being on the sauce for a few weeks were horrendous. I saw him on the deck one day just after a crew change and when I jumped out from behind him for a joke he almost had a heart attack, among other things. There were a few of us who used to sit and nurse a pint at Stavanger airport, at £6 a time, until we boarded the flight home. Derrick man Les Liddell, from Aberdeen, would not spend a penny at the airport and would wander about for sometimes two hours rather than spend £6 on a beer. So there we all are, some nursing a beer, another wandering about telling us how daft we were paying £6 for a pint, and Alex getting wired in. The survival suits in the Norwegian sector, which you must wear for travelling offshore and back onshore, were brilliant and if anything did happen with a helicopter accident and you were to survive, these would definitely give you a fair chance of surviving in the North Sea. The UK sector survival suits at the time were poor - you could then spit peas through them and we often remarked that they were just a body bag. The Norwegian ones were huge, fully quilted and had little wellington boots fully attached. The bold Alex did not tell anyone but in his rush to the heliport he lost his shoes. Not to be beaten he borrowed a pair of scissors or a knife and cut the boots from his survival suit. He had kept his feet tucked under the table at the bar during our wait, but when nature called and he had to go to the toilet you can imagine the comments when off he toddles with little bright red wellington boots on, that you could clearly see had been cut from his survival suit. Now if the drinks were not expensive enough you can imagine his face when he was handed the bill on next trip back to the rig for the damage for repairing the survival suit.

I continued to take advantage of any courses that were going. Stena Drilling were brilliant about any courses you wanted to attend that would benefit the rig and yourself. You just put it past the office and got the go-ahead. I studied NEEBOSH General Safety Certification on my time off at Stevenson's College in Edinburgh, and it was when enlisting for an Offshore Crane Inspection training course in Aberdeen that things really took a twist. I had studied all about the different standards regarding safety offshore and indeed other UK lifting regulations. What put an idea in my head was that on one recent trip there were Inspectors from DNV (Den Norske Veritas) on the rig to inspect the cranes and I thought to myself 'I could do this'. I asked around about what qualifications you needed to become an inspector and drew a blank. Peter Armstrong did say one thing that stuck with me, '…it is not really all that much of a big deal Craig'.

On the second day of the Offshore Crane Inspection course, the instructor asked me to stay behind at break time for a few moments. He asked me where I worked and where I had learned all the knowledge from. I told him I worked in Norway on the two-three, two-four rotation, and was studying safety during my time off. This was to be another piece of the jigsaw.

'Would you fancy being an Instructor during your time off, working for me?' he asked.

I explained that I would rather head down the safety way or indeed Inspection.

'Well I pay £180 per day if you were to become interested' he added.

Now this was in 1990. Not a bad day rate and my ears started to ring with numbers. The thing was that I never did any work for this instructor as he ran a very shabby operation, but it certainly gave me food for thought. I did drive up to Aberdeen at one point to speak to him about 'train the trainer' training, but did not feel comfortable at all with him or his partner. Here I was sitting in their office and they were quite prepared to send me offshore with no formal training to conduct a Banksman/Slinger training course. There was no way I was going. On my way out of his office I met a guy called David Richards who did work for these people. Now he had heard these guys talking about me and asked if I would have a chat with him on the phone later. David Richards contacted me a few days later and informed me that he was starting his own training company and that he no longer wished to work for this shabby outfit in Aberdeen. He added that I had done the correct thing by walking away from them. If I was interested in his offer, he invited me to attend a full five-day course on Train the Trainer in Hull. This was another feather in my cap as this was an interesting and very enjoyable course. It was also provided free of charge by David Richards. He even provided accommodation at a local hotel. After completing the course he then asked me if I would be interested in going to an old Penrod Drilling rig, offshore Blackpool, to conduct a Banksman/Slinger training course. My reply was let me get my next trip on board Dyvi Stena out of the way and will be available as soon as I get home.

He was good to his word, and after being home for a few days I contacted David Richards to see if the training assignment onboard Penrod 80 was still going to happen.

'Get yourself prepared, you will be going very shortly', came his reply.

I drove down to Blackpool and took the helicopter out from the airport to Morecambe Bay gas fields. I was nervous, but confident I could deliver what was required. The Penrod 80 was a small Jack Up drilling rig with an elderly American guy in charge. He acted as both OIM and senior tool pusher. I remember this guy as he had a lot of bother with his ears and was often seen borrowing caustic soda from the mud engineer to put in his ears with a toothpick. He reckoned it temporarily cleared the wax problem. Now if you look up caustic soda on the internet you will see that it removes more than wax. A dangerous act, and no wonder he was short of hearing.

I explained to him what would be best for the training schedule, and things went well. I recommended the theory part for things which should be done when the guys were off shift and the practical exercises when they were on shift. If things were quiet on board I suggested conducting everything when the guys were on shift. The area manager for Penrod Drilling came out to the rig as he was alarmed by the amount of silly little accidents they were having on board. I never forgot James Broyles as I was going to bump into him quite a few times over the following years. James sat in on one of my classes and after I had finished, he informed me that I was doing well and to keep up the good work. These encouraging words were very welcomed, and I had a sense of achieving something as well as enjoying conducting the training. Before I knew it, I was booked to return to the Penrod 80 to conduct Banksman/Slinger training for the other two crews who were at home when I had conducted training on my first visit. The reports David Richards received from the rig were glowing, and the Penrod 80 insisted that it would be me who returned to complete the training. I was delighted with the report and my start to training.

After completing the Penrod 80 training, another job for David Richards came up off-shore in Denmark (Esbjerg) for Smedvig. The weather had been shocking with fog and there were no flights or helicopters moving. The rig manager for one of these rigs was a chap called Les Thomas. With hotels being heavily booked he asked if I would mind sharing a room with the rig welder from Edinburgh, who was also a new hire. He explained that it would only be for a couple of nights until the fog cleared. I did not mind sharing, as I was earning good money on top of my salary and I enjoyed conducting the training.

After a few beers too many and something to eat I headed for bed. Early the next morning the phone in the room rang. I didn't answer it but after a while the rig welder suggested we should. I said that it wouldn't be for me, more likely some joker, so he should just tell them where to go. The rig welder answered and told the caller to 'fuck off'. Well, all hell broke loose. Our room door almost collapsed inwards with the thumping of a fist on the door. It was the rig manager, and to say he was not pleased would have been understatement of the year! The fog had cleared and he wanted everyone ready to go to the heliport immediately. I did not do myself any favours there and word got back to David Richards that I had been out all night and had told the rig manager to 'fuck off'! This of course was rubbish. I completed the training as requested but could sense that David, who did not even ask for my side of events, may not use me again.

The thing is, I really enjoyed what I was doing and in the back of my mind always knew Norway would not last forever. Once home I sat down with Judith and suggested that I start my own business.

'Norway will not last forever and you have experience doing accounts', I reasoned.

We both agreed it was a gamble and with a youngster to bring up, it was even more risky, but we thought 'why not'.

Chapter 4

JCD Crane Services is born

Returning to the Dyvi Stena, it would be my last trip onboard. The Russian Jack up 'Kolskaya', translated into English as 'Big Island', required an operator for a week as the Icelandic operator they had on board was not very good and rather reckless on the controls. These cranes were more like an onshore mobile crane with telescopic panel booms, unlike I had ever seen previously offshore. Reckless is possibly a bit mild here for describing the operator as the rig welder spent most of his time following him around the rig, patching up the damage. The last straw apparently was when he tried to land a large load of pipe work on the helideck, ripped up the netting and when this failed to work, he tried to control the load by landing it in the water. The plan was for me to do one week on board Dyvi Stena then one-week on board Kolskaya and then home. There were still a few Russians onboard when I arrived and the stories were quite fresh how these guys had never seen a full complement of catering crew onboard a rig before. They were used to going to a hatch and receiving a lunch box during meal breaks, and whatever was inside you ate. They were all apparently amazed when the Norwegian catering crew arrived onboard. For once they could actually serve themselves from an actual menu in the galley! Some of them had never seen oranges or bananas before. I'm not sure if that is true, but you could see the novelty for them of eating good food in the galley. I was also told that the Russian crew wasn't used to having their work clothes washed, cabins cleaned and beds changed also. One of the rig mechanics, who spoke good English, was an interesting person to speak with as he was very open about life in communist Russia. He explained how people used to just queue at a shop to see what was for sale, everyone had money he reckoned as they had nothing to spend it on.

The trip passed quickly and before I knew it, I was back home to start planning the launch of JCD Crane Services. I had five years' service with Dyvi Stena and after a good number of phone calls back and forward between Scotland and Norway, I negotiated a redundancy package. In the background, the rig was getting very top heavy with UK personnel and they had hinted that anyone with five years' service could be eligible for a redundancy package. I contacted the local Job Centre at home and another good leg up here was the £40 a week start up allowance from the government. I qualified for this and it was a godsend as you received this for six months. At least we were not going to starve.

To get everything in to place I then booked myself on a ten-day course in Falkirk to become an RTITB (Road Transport Industry Training Board) Forklift Truck Examiner. Every oil rig has forklift trucks onboard and I knew this was going to be a key service to offer, and I could also conduct courses onshore at factories. I then contacted the CITB (Construction Industry Training Board) to become a recognised crane Instructor. They were the only people in the world at that time who had recognised crane instructors. I joined them for a Crawler Crane Instructor course as this was the closest thing to an Offshore Marine Crane. With the above in place I maybe should have moved to Aberdeen but instead decided to keep going in Selkirk and travel to where I was required. JCD Crane Services were now able to offer: Banksman/Slinger training or as I called it Slinger/Signaller, Forklift Truck Operator training, Crawler Crane Operator training, and Offshore Crane Operator training.

As my gut feeling told me, I was in the right place at the right time as there were not a lot of people in the training business. There was plenty to build on.

I telephoned Penrod Drilling in Great Yarmouth and asked to speak with James Broyles, informing him that I had now started my own business and would he consider giving me a chance. I could not believe my ears.

'Speak with my secretary, Hailey, you will be going to the Penrod 85 on Monday, she will arrange helicopter and speak with the rig. Please conduct all the training you can'.

That was the start. It was music to my ears. During the remainder of 1991 and a part of 1992 I conducted training onboard the Penrod 80, 85 and 92. Eventually, Penrod Drilling sold all their rigs to a new company in the offshore drilling business called Ensco and JCD Crane Services were going to be part of the training on board all of their rigs. This was going to be further down the road and will come back into my story a little later. In the meantime, it was a case of searching and finding new clients to offer training on board their installations and of course any factories onshore requiring FLT Operator training.

Our son Iain was born in March 1992, and as far as I was concerned one of each, a daughter and a son, was enough for anyone to be going on with. This also spurned me on to find new work. I landed lucky with a paper mill about 45 minutes' drive from home and found myself there for six weeks solid, conducting five-day forklift courses. I also landed lucky with a company about 18 miles from home where they had a requirement for FLT training as well as two old Ruston Bucyrus Crawler cranes (19 RB and 21 RB). These were for loading finished storage tanks onto trailers for delivery and for turning the tanks during manufacture. The manager at this factory informed me that we could use the cranes for training if needed, as they were not used all that much. With me using them for training ensured they would be well maintained. These old cranes, if not well maintained, seize up very quickly. My business was progressing well, and while not making a fortune I had enough work to be going on with.

During this same stime I picked up a training project offshore from Aberdeen. It was a small job on a rig called the Kan Tan IV, that had been sold and was going to China. Why they were going to conduct training onboard a rig going to China baffled me, but money is money, and I decided that there was going to be far too much work for one Instructor. This was my first step at hiring in a sub-contracted Instructor. I hired an Instructor from Peterhead who had been on the Train the Trainer course in Hull. Peter Fellows had the same idea as me but for some reason did not follow it up and he was quite happy with an odd job here and there and this project suited him well.

We landed onboard the Kan Tan IV and to say we were surplus to requirement was an understatement. Nobody, and I am talking nobody, wanted us there. We tried our best to conduct training but you were no sooner starting a class when the OIM would take everyone out of the class. On one occasion the assistant rig manager removed all the guys from one of the courses that Peter was conducting for no apparent reason. The personnel on board had a terrible attitude - I have never experienced anything like it. We were conducting a course when all the roustabouts stated very clearly to us, 'look, we are fisherman, we are only here for another ten days and will not be back... we are not interested in your training'.

'And you are not from Aberdeen, trainers should be from Aberdeen'.

To make matters worse when the bacon rolls were being served in the coffee shop at break time, these guys were certainly not happy at Peter and I having any.

'These rolls are not for you, they are for us'.

My patience started to wear a bit thin, and when an ignorant OIM made a remark that we should be doing more training, I asked him, 'how can we conduct a training course when you keep taking participants away?'

I spoke with their office in Aberdeen but everything appeared to fall on deaf ears. As if the above was not enough they hired us again to return for a final visit. The last straw for me doing work offshore Aberdeen was when Peter arrived in the morning with an eye that looked as though he had been in the ring with Mike Tyson.

'Managed to get into a bit of an argument in a bar last night' he explained.

You can imagine my thoughts. We were heading out to a rig where we were not welcome and one of the Instructors could hardly open one of his eyes. To be very fair the second visit was nowhere near as bad as first, but I was certainly glad to see the back end of that job. When Peter told me he was going to concentrate on his bed-and-breakfast business we shook hands and parted company. I never saw or heard of Peter again after that project.

Chapter 5

First taste of South East Asia and an extremely serious accident

I received an enquiry in December 1992 about perhaps going to a project in West Malaysia. The company was called Atwood Oceanic (bought over by Ensco years later). It was an old drilling contractor from the States, and most of their rigs were named after famous battles during the American Civil War, such as Vicksburg and Gettysburg. One of the company's old semi submersibles that had worked in Australia for years called the Margie, after one of owner's daughters, had been converted to a Drill Assist Tender.

The question was put to me… 'as you are a registered Crane Instructor would you be interested in going offshore Kuala Terengganu, West Malaysia for a month to supervise the heavy lifts onboard the new tender as a new crane had been installed and the drill packages were quite heavy?'

These tenders are used to go alongside a small platform that has no accommodation, and all the drilling package is lifted on board the platform. Decks are used on board and everyone sleeps and eats on board the tender. Once all drilling is finished everything is then removed from the unmanned platform back onto the tender and she is then off to her next assignment. She is also towed by tugs as she did not have her own engines, I hasten to add.

Day rates were agreed for my services and I travelled to Kuala Lumpur in early January 1993, on what I thought would be a new and exciting chapter. Once I landed in KL, I was taken to a hotel for the night before flying onto Kuantan in West Malaysia, and then by road to Kuala Terengganu. I checked in to the hotel and had a shower, a bite to eat and then got my head down after the long flight from the UK. I was just dozing off when I heard someone open the hotel room door. I jumped out of bed to be met by an Australian barge master, who was travelling to the Seahawk. I asked the old guy if he had got the wrong room.

'No', was the reply, 'Atwood make us guys share a room'.

38

I should have seen the writing on the wall at this point. The old barge captain snored all night. We made our way early in the morning back to the airport for a domestic flight to Kuantan and were driven to Atwood base before getting a helicopter out to the rig. I met the manager, whose first words were, 'what are we doing with a North Sea wanker down here... we not got anyone from Australia?' Charming.

I arrived on the tender and it could only be described as a war zone. The barge was nowhere near ready to be on location and there were shipyard projects still going on and boxes with equipment scattered everywhere. Everyone was running around like headless chickens – all of them shit-frightened of this area manager in town.

The cranes were in poor condition. The old link belt construction cranes had simply been taken from their under carriage (tracks) and put on a pedestal. It was the same scenario as the Sinbad in the North Sea, and this certainly benefited me. To make matters worse, though, it was still the monsoon season offshore here, and when it rained, boy did it rain. The gale-force winds didn't help either. I watched the local operator, who could have been Malaysian or Indonesian, operating one of the cranes and noted he had a little plastic bucket full of barite next to him - barite mixed with water is the main ingredient for making mud to pump down a well by the way. It was a very primitive operator's cabin, and when I asked him what the barite was for, he firstly tried to dismiss he understood, but then when he was coming up and down with the hook I noticed him throwing barite onto the space between the wire rope drum and brake pad. The wire rope drum was next to him at the operator's seat. With the monsoon weather, when the drum was wet it could not hold the load, therefore the operator threw barite in between the drum and brake band as it acted as a grip to ensure the brake actually worked and the load did not slip. Never mind primitive, this was like something from Noah's Ark. Next up was this new crane that had just been installed. I wish I had met the salesman who sold Atwood this crane, I would have offered him a job selling my training immediately. Now this crane was diesel hydraulic (diesel engine being the prime mover to power the main hydraulic pump and hydraulic motors). Usually the slew ring, that enables the crane to rotate, is a toothed pinion that meshes with a toothed slew ring, either internally or externally on the pedestal. These also have an internal roller ball type load bearing where the crane is attached to the pedestal with huge bolts. But not on this crane. It was chain driven and I could see the crane had already snapped the chain when the operator was obviously trying to control a load by slewing either left or right quickly to control the load. It was the worst design I have ever seen.

Preparations were going ahead to lift the huge drilling draw works from the tender up to the platform. This was a lift that would be in the region of 60 tonnes. Anyway, with myself being there as a lift supervisor and with the state of this tender and the cranes, I informed them that they were asking for trouble. I said I was against this lift even being contemplated until at least the weather calmed down. I also asked how they could trust this new crane with a lift like this? A few phone calls to the area manager and I was overruled. Surely the oil company must step in, but they never did. Neither did the safety officer on board. To ensure I was a safe distance away and up high where I could see all that was going on, I made my way onto a stack of pipe work with boxes and pieces of wood lying all over the place. The local operator was lifting some boxes or something nearby and I also kept my eye on this. I did not realise at the time, but he apparently managed to get a sling caught under some wood quite close to where I was standing, and instead of getting a roustabout to pull the sling clear he simply pulled up the hook when the sling freed itself. It moved the pipe work and pieces of wood and threw me backwards to fall between pipe work and wooden boxes. I must have fallen backwards five or six feet. The pain, especially on my lower back was excruciating, and with being winded I also vomited. I'm not sure, but I also think I briefly passed out. I don't know how long it was before crew managed to get me out but I had been very lucky, as my safety helmet had fallen off and my head had missed a valve by inches on the way down. Where I landed there was also a piece of wood with a large nail sticking out. I was stretchered into the medical room. The pain in my lower back, with being moved from the deck, was like nothing I had ever felt before. I am not sure how long I was there when the door burst open and it was the old barge captain and a few other

40

guys coming for the stretcher. I could not pick up exactly what he yelled, but it was something like 'you are in good shape compared to the rig superintendent'. I found out later that they had gone ahead with the lift that I told them not to attempt, and without sounding like a 'told you so', they had tried to lift the draw works and this crane had yet again broke its chain on the slew. The operator could do nothing but watch the load rotate on its own. The rig superintendent tried to grab one of the tag lines and it simply flipped him up in the air like a rag doll. He had a serious head injury. The emergency helicopter was sent for and before I knew it, the two of us were medically evacuated to hospital. He was slipping in and out of consciousness, and with the movement of the helicopter yet again the pain in my lower back was excruciating. We arrived at a primitive hospital with the cockroaches wandering about the floors - some were so big they acted as nurses. Every now again the rig superintendent would regain consciousness and repeat, 'this is the big apple you know, the big apple', before drifting off again. It was alarming lying there in a lot of pain and nobody offering you anything to help. I managed to get to the toilet at one stage, but the pain was terrible. Once I saw the state of the toilets I did not want to go back in a hurry. A representative from Atwood came to the hospital in the morning and after seeing the state of the place asked if I would be better in a hotel. I said that if the doctor was happy with me going, I would like to. I cannot remember if the rig superintendent was also moved to a hotel. The Atwood representative came and visited a few times and every time would ask if he could book me on a helicopter back to the rig. That was all he was interested in. My answer was always the same.

'How can I travel back to the rig in this state? I can hardly move and the pain is simply unbearable at times. Is there not a doctor anywhere?'

There was no doctor, apparently. After a few days the representative sent an Indian warehouseman to simply spy on me. I never thought much about it at the time, but he would come up to my room to ask me how I was and ask if I played darts.

'Would you fancy a game?'

'Listen mate', I said, 'I'm not sure what is going on here, but I am not interested in playing darts. I simply want a doctor as I can hardly go to the toilet, let alone walk.'

All my meals were brought to me by room service, but sitting up to try and eat was difficult. Sleeping was another issue. If I turned slightly, the agony kicked in again.

After another couple of days, the same Atwood representative returned to inform that the operations manager was coming by and would I consider going back to the rig. You can guess my answer to that one, and once the operations manager came round things really got nasty.

'Will you go back to the rig to recover?'

'NO!'

'Okay, I am sending you to a hospital in Kuala Lumpur where they will scan you and if I am correct and they inform me there is nothing wrong with you, I will sack you and start legal proceedings against you.'

I could not believe my ears. Here I was thousands of miles from home, stuck in a hotel in a lot of pain and having to listen to this bastard.

'I am ready to go as soon as you organise a flight', I stated.

He stormed out the room muttering, 'What are we doing with this fucking North Sea wanker anyway'.

I felt like telling him what I thought of him and his shabby operation, but I decided to keep quiet and wait until a better opportunity came up. When you are lying in a lot of pain in a bed, it is not the best time to get into a war of words. The minibus journey to Kuantan airport and the flight to Kuala Lumpur were simply horrendous. I have ever had pain like this - sometimes it would ease slightly, but the slightest movement and it was like a hot knife going into the bottom of my back. It also felt like pieces of sharp glass floating around my lower spine. I thought at one point that I was going to pass out! I finally made it to the hospital and compared to the previous place, this was like a palace. As soon as the doctor saw me, he informed me that I looked in bad shape and would be going for an MRI scan in the morning. He also prescribed morphine to help me with the pain and get a night's sleep. He could not believe that the accident had happened almost a week earlier.

He shook his head, stating: 'you should have been here days ago.'

When the morphine kicked in, it was honestly like heaven for those first moments to be pain free. It felt like I was floating on top of the bed.

I have never had an MRI scan before and when I first saw this tube that they were going to push me into, I wondered what was going on.

'Just relax and it will be all over soon', they explained.

It only took around 10 minutes, and when I was being pushed out of the MRI room one of the assistants said that I would not be going anywhere fast. Once I was back to the bed the doctor came round with the prognosis.

'Your back is not broken, but you have two slipped discs - L4 and L5 - and L3 is showing a slight bulge. We will give you pain killers and shall put you onto traction with weights at the bottom of the bed to try and relieve the pressure on your discs.'

After a few days the doctor asked me if I would consider surgery as he had a very good German surgeon who would simply trim the discs.

'No thanks' was my immediate answer. There was no way I was having anyone cut into my back. All I wanted to do was get better or be in good enough shape to fly home.

According to my old passports I arrived in Malaysia on the 6th January, 1993 and returned to the UK on the 25th January. In between these dates most of my time was spent in hospital recovering. When they eventually flew me home it was perhaps a bit soon. As my ticket was economy, the journey took its toll, and when arriving in London I was in agony. I still had the flight to Edinburgh and the car journey home to Selkirk. Once home I spent a week lying on the floor strapped into a surgical corset and lying on a cloth cylinder to help my back. I was taken to Borders General Hospital for physiotherapy where they had a good aqua pool. The heat in the pool was immense and it certainly did the trick. I could finally feel myself starting to get better.

Before I finish this chapter, I have to inform you what I found out in later years about what happened to the rig superintendent. He had suffered a fractured skull and his skull was leaking fluid. He apparently died of his injuries about a year after the incident, poor fellow. Various operators were tried, but all in vain. As for the operations manager, he was sacked by Atwood Oceanic at a conference dinner for higher management in Houston, Texas. He was apparently a rotten drunk and tried to have a go at the other people in higher management and the big boss sacked him on the spot. I also found out that it was not the first time he had been involved in an accident on one of his rigs. On an earlier occasion a poor fellow had died instantly, and it wasn't long before the bold operations manager was round at the widow's house asking her not to sue the company. I also found out that this unsavoury character died of liver cancer. I do not think there would be many shedding tears at his burial. I certainly would not have been!

Chapter 6

Convalescing and looking for new contracts

I spent a good part of early 1993 recovering from the slipped discs but with the good physiotherapy and use of the hydrotherapy pool I was gradually able to put this unpleasant time behind me and get back into looking for new training projects. Thankfully, it did not take long before I secured a good one.

Judith answered the first phone call from a rig manager called Minos Landry from a company called Rowan Drilling, who had a few rigs offshore Yarmouth in the Southern Sector of the North Sea. I had already conducted training for Penrod Drilling off Yarmouth and word must have made it to their neighbour's office. When I contacted Minos, he asked if I would be interested in conducting training for Rowan Drilling.

'No problem' was my immediate reply.

He was a smashing old guy, originally from Greece and had immigrated to America years ago. Every now and again I could hear the Greek accent but most of the time he spoke with the US southern drawl. The first rig I worked onboard for Rowan was the Arch Rowan. Rowan Drilling are a very old American drilling contractor, and at one time when they first started drilling in UK waters they used to have their own aircraft and used to fly everyone across from the States - the drill crew, the marine crew and even the catering crew! They even had a good share in the Marathon Le Tourneau shipyard in the States, where all their rigs were built. These rigs were not designed for comfort, but they were certainly good work horses. The British guys who at this point worked for them had all been there for a few years and although Rowan did not pay the biggest salaries in the world, they took great pride in never laying anyone off, even if a rig was stacked (not working , no contract). It meant that if a rig was not working the crew were all onboard constantly doing maintenance and painting work. As soon as a job came up on the horizon with an oil company, they were in the good position of being ready to go in a very short period of time, while other drilling contractors would need to crew up, and prepare the rig. This certainly gave Rowan Drilling an advantage when looking for contracts. The list of training requirements was quite extensive, and it meant new courses would need to be developed. Two of these were Offshore Helicopter Landing Officer and Offshore Helicopter Refuelling courses. They had previously had some near misses with helicopters in this zone; one of them being with the earth wire that is attached to the helicopter from the rig by crocodile type clips when refuelling. On one occasion they had forgotten to remove the earth wire after refuelling a helicopter and the helicopter landing officer unfortunately failed to notice until it was too late. As the helicopter departed the rig it simply ripped the wire and reel attached from the helideck. Flying back to North Denes heliport with this the reel and wire dangling underneath the helicopter took a bit of explaining once the pilot landed. If the wire had flipped round to the rotor blades it could have been a very nasty accident.

On one crew change apparently the pilot was getting ready to take off when one of the helideck crew was still inside the luggage hold under the helicopter. Another lucky escape! I remember on one refuelling course it was a bit wet and windy on the helideck to be showing the deck crew about testing JET A1 fuel for cleanliness and very importantly testing for any water contamination. I decided to move inside to the recreation room that we used as a classroom for all theory parts of the courses. Some of the participants on this particular course were from an area in Great Yarmouth called Galston. They weren't the brightest buttons in the box. I started explaining about JET A1 fuel and how dangerous it is and very flammable, and I had the large glass jar with me in the classroom full of the fuel. One of the participants reached into his pocket and removed a cigarette from a packet. I stopped talking but his buddy next to him suddenly turned around and I expected he was going to tell him off about the dangers of flames and fuel, but no… he asked him for a smoke. Thankfully, the others in the class came to my rescue!

The training was going very well with the Arch Rowan, and as soon as the first two crews were finished, I received a booking to return and catch the other two crews. The crews on second visit were mainly from Liverpool. It was a bit like the Liverpool mafia onboard as they certainly outnumbered personnel from any other part of the UK. I found them to be very humorous and I liked their craic. There was one big family of Scousers on board and the younger brother was, we shall say, a wee bit slow. These are the days before power point presentations and all theory parts of classes were conducted with slides on a projector. On a forklift truck course I showed the figures from the UK on the fatalities from related accidents in a five year period. At that time there had been approximately 65 fatalities in a five-year period. When I asked if there were any questions before moving on, the above lad says to me, 'Craig, those fatalities, are those the deaths as well?' The place was in uproar with laughter!

When I finished the Arch Rowan, I received the good news that the other rigs working in the area were also interested in hiring me! It was music to my ears. I conducted training for Rowan Drilling onboard the Rowan Californian, the Rowan Halifax, the Cecile Provine, the Charles Rowan and the Gorilla IV. I recently found out that all of these rigs, after finishing in the North Sea because of their old age, ended up in Saudi Arabia, working for Saudi Aramco. Coincidentally I found out this information from my son Iain when he started off in the oil industry as a lifting gear and offshore crane inspector. He visited them all on numerous occasions and he often remarked about the poor condition of the accommodation. It was the same as all those years before when I visited them - work horses indeed but comfortable accommodation I am afraid not.

Dan Coco was the rig manager of the Rowan Californian and this is when yet again another course was going to have to be developed.

'Craig, could you put together a scaffold course for my hands?'

'Let me get onto it' was my reply.

With my safety background I knew the scaffold regulations, but I wasn't competent at erecting and dismantling scaffold systems. Enter Alexander 'Barker' Bruce; a good old friend of mine who is a genius with scaffolding. Barker is originally from Selkirk too and he had learned his trade in London. More importantly, he was a certified advanced scaffolder with the CITB in the UK. After over 25 years in London, Barker had returned home and we met in Selkirk. We started to put a plan together that included sending scaffold materials and scaffold tools to the rig. I would take care of the theory and assist Barker with the practical exercises. I contacted the CITB for assistance and also spoke with the National Access and Scaffolding Confederation. The CITB have their own competency programmes for scaffolding, level 1, level 2 and advanced, but fully understood that these participants were all oil field people and their training scheme was not suitable. I sent Barker to Aberdeen for his RGIT Offshore Survival and Offshore medical. All was going to plan until on the morning of our departure for Norwich from Edinburgh. Barker suddenly went quiet. What he did not inform me of was that he had not flown for years and was rather reluctant to fly! After a bit of coaxing and persuasion I managed to get the Barker onto the flight. This course turned out to be a winner! I remember meeting a barge engineer from the very first course many years later in Thailand and one of the first things he said was that he had 'never forgotten the scaffold course'.

He added, 'I did an extension to my house and did not need a scaffolding company as I never forgot what you both taught us and it saved me a small fortune. I hired the material myself and with help of a friend erected and dismantled the scaffold on my own'.

Who says training does not pay!

The word back from the rig was also encouraging and before I knew it, we were booked back again as Rowan started saving quite a bit of money with having their own team onboard. I have to emphasis here that there was no over the side work and this was only for basic scaffold projects. It was a good feather in my cap but selling this course did not happen overnight. Over the years (1994 to 2005) we conducted scaffold courses in Qatar, Thailand, Singapore, Nigeria and Argentina.

It was around this time that music was becoming more and more available on satellite television and I remember Barker and I sitting in the TV room at a break time onboard the Rowan Californian listening to BB King. An American tool pusher came into the room, grabbed the remote and switched the TV off, stating very loudly, 'get that shit off'. I could not believe it! I found out later that night that the USA drill crew would always be away at meetings and nobody was allowed to go near these. I did not think much about it at the time as I thought it was just drilling business, but in fact they were Ku Klux Klan meetings. This explained the dislike of BB King and his brilliant music!

Around this time, I also found out that Penrod Drilling had been sold to a company called Ensco, who not a lot of people, including myself, had heard anything about. I tried contacting James Broyles but found out that he had serious health problems, was returning to the USA for a liver transplant and was retiring from the oil industry. Barker went back to his self-employed scaffolder status at home in the Borders and I assured him not to worry, for as soon as we got the nod for another job I would be back in touch immediately. Little did I know then that this course was a winner for sure.

Chapter 7

Back to South East Asia

By casting my net far and wide, I found a fax one morning from a training company in Sarawak, Malaysia. It asked if I would be interested in conducting training for them in Singapore, and when finished, if I would travel to the training centre in Miri, Sarawak. Surely, after what had happened with Atwood, lightning could not strike twice. It was approximately a six week job. 'Why not', I thought, and off I went to Singapore. The first project was with the crane operators from a company called OPI, who are no longer with us. They had pipe laying vessels and heavy lift barges, which were all old but did a job. Everything was well organised, from the pick-up at the airport in Singapore to the hotel where I would be staying, and the transport back and forward to the shipyard. I also noted how clean the place was. It was more like a European city than one in South East Asia, and everyone spoke English or as the Singaporeans refer to it, 'Senglish'. 'Okay la!' Every sentence appeared to end with 'okay la'. When arriving at the shipyard off Pioneer Road and seeing the crane on board the Technic Padu, DLB 264, I realised it was unlike anything I had seen before. It was a huge crane. I spoke with management and the HSE manager, Stuart Meachen, who I would meet many times again over the years. I explained that, 'yes, I am a qualified crane instructor with CITB from the UK, but I have never seen anything like this'. As we were not on a tight schedule I asked if it would be possible to spend time with an experienced operator and see for myself what was involved with operating a crane of this size. It was all agreed and I spent two days with two experienced operators ahead of training, and what an experience this was. The main block (hook) weighed 32 tonnes. There was approximately five miles of rope on the four drums, and the boom was huge, weighing over 300 tonnes. The full-time oiler, as they called the fellow in the engine house, ensured nothing went wrong and kept all the greasing and maintenance up to date. The crane was an old Clyde AM model and was originally built in 1968. I really enjoyed operating this crane and used to say to myself, 'well if I ever end up bankrupt I know what direction I will be going in'. The work rotation for these operators, though, might not have suited me - ninety days on and thirty off. It was really like operating three cranes as each hook has individual controls. When rotating the crane it felt like huge rail carriage wheels that rotated round a path instead of your usual slew ring. On the second day they allowed me to lift a steam hammer, as they called it. Everything, as you can well imagine, on a crane of this magnitude is seriously planned and is slow and carefully lifted. When looking at the load indicator it showed 250 tonnes. Yet here was this old crane picking up this steam hammer without the slightest difficulty. It was an enjoyable experience.

I met the crews that were to receive training, and this was my first experience with Iban tribesman from Sarawak. They were the best riggers I have ever seen. They were great people to have in your team. The DLB 264 was side by side with another pipe laying barge, the DLB 332, on the quayside. Next to them was a metal cage with two snakes inside - one a large python and the other a smaller black snake, apparently from Brunei. Shipyards are terrible for rats and the Iban guys would catch the rats and drop them into the cage. The rat would just sit there for a day or two, cowering in the corner, knowing that its fate was coming as soon as one of these snakes was hungry. I would have an occasional look in the cage and, sure enough, there would be no rats, just two fat snakes. They ate them whole, apparently, even the smaller snake. There was never a shortage of rats for the Iban to feed their snakes.

After finishing my first hitch in Singapore it was onto Miri in Sarawak, Borneo. Miri is an old oil town. Royal Dutch Shell drilled a well there as far back as 1910. It was a different experience being on hire to another training provider, but certainly enjoyable and another great experience. Weekends were okay in Miri and I did plenty exploring as I was only working Monday to Friday. My translator was keen to show me a Long House, and with transport organised we set off into the Borneo jungle early one Saturday morning. These wooden houses on stilts were the original homes of the tribespeople all

51

those years ago. They were long wooden shacks, like giant hen houses with different families having different rooms, and the chief of the tribe in the biggest room. One of the tribespeople showed me a suitcase full of shrunken skulls from retreating Japanese soldiers in World War II. These people still detested the Japanese as many of their forefathers were murdered by the soldiers when they first invaded Sarawak. It was a different story at the end of the war, with the tribespeople enjoying payback time as the Japanese soldiers retreated through the jungle.

'The Gurkha soldier is not good - he is too noisy with big boots. The Japanese hear them coming and hide. They cannot hide from us - we carefully hide in undergrowth and hit them with blow pipe' I was informed by my translator.

These blow pipes have darts that are very poisonous with a venom tip. They kill you in no time. The translator also told me that representatives of the Japanese government had visited the village to request the return of the remains of the Japanese soldiers, but these people were having none of it. The shrunken skulls were staying in Borneo.

While in Miri at the training centre, the company had me staying in a hotel called the Pacific Orient. It was very much an oil field hotel then with a 24-hour coffee shop. An American, who was the boss of an oil field service company, had his people living in the hotel and he complained bitterly to the staff about the state of this coffee shop in the mornings. With being open all night, when his guys were coming down for breakfast it was a right mess. At the same time as this guy was complaining, apparently the Malaysian mafia were in town looking for someone high up on their hit list. They searched everywhere and were getting ready to give up the search when they decided that a coffee was in order, They made for the 24-hour coffee shop in the Pacific Orient. Low and behold, the guy they were looking for was sitting in the coffee shop. Now, these people are not the type you would take home to meet your mother, and armed with parangs, which is Malaysian for machetes, these gangsters cut this guy to pieces and fled quickly. After the police had been involved and removed all the remains, the staff cleaned the place up immaculately. A few hours later, enter the American who immediately began praising the staff for listening to him and for cleaning the coffee shop. Little did he know that a few hours earlier a guy had been chopped to pieces just yards from where he was standing.

I did a couple of trips offshore while on hire for this training provider to old rigs, the Charley Graves, an old drill-assist tender barge, and the Randolph Yost, an old jack up drilling rig. The drilling contractor was Reading and Bates, an old company who were eventually taken over by a larger consortium. The mud engineer onboard the Randolph Yost remembered me from the Dyvi Stena and it was good at night time talking to him about past experiences in Norway. I will always remember his words, 'South East Asia for me for now on - no more North Sea'. Unfortunately, I did not ever meet him again as he died of the dreaded cancer.

My second visit to Singapore in June 1994, was much the same as the last trip, except I found a grand little bar not far from Orchard Road and the Lady Hill Hotel where I was staying. The Cave Man Bar was run by two shipyard boys from Singapore as their part-time earner at nights. It was a great little bar and cheap for Singapore. You would get all sorts of people in the bar for the craic. I was standing one night when this guy next to me asked what part of Scotland I was from. He was originally from Dunfermline in Fife. He had married a Filipino, and he told me, and had never been back home for years. John Mather was a second engineer onboard a BP oil tanker and was in Singapore for a court case. There had been a serious accident in one of the shipyards on board the ship he was working on. It was a confined space entry accident, where a welder had started his torch next to some painters and almost blew the ship out of the water! Many people had been killed or injured and John was in town to give evidence. He was on his own, the same as myself, and asked if it was okay to meet at nights as he would be in town for a few days. I was delighted as he was good company and I could speak in my native tongue. The reason for recounting this incident was later in the year, after finishing off training in Malaysia, I was at home when Judith wanted to do some Christmas shopping at the Gyle Centre in Edinburgh. I was sitting outside a shop when an Asian girl walked past me. At this time in my career could not tell the difference between Malaysian, Filipino, Indonesian or Thai, but when I looked again here was this guy with her and I thought that looks like John Mather who I had met in Singapore. I gave him a nod of the head and said, 'Caveman Bar'. As sure as hell, it was John! BP, after the court case, were sending all their personnel to Aberdeen for fire -fighting training and here he was in Edinburgh after visiting his mother in Dunfermline.

Chapter 8

Indonesia

Early in 1995 I was shaking the apple tree yet again to see what work would drop my way. I had previously been in contact with Dolphin Drilling in Aberdeen, who was owned by the shipping magnate Fred Olsen, He wanted out of the oil business but his daughter disagreed and she was in charge of the drilling company. The HR department contacted me asking if I would be interested in travelling to Indonesia to visit the Byford Dolphin, an old semi-submersible drilling rig that had worked down in the southern hemisphere for quite a while. Forklift truck training was the initial request but as it was a long way to go and the training was mainly for the locals, they requested that I stay on board for twenty eight days and conduct as much training as I possibly could. With the price agreed I sent my passport to Dolphin Drilling who in turn sent it to the Indonesian Embassy in London for a work permit and visa. After quite a wait, my passport was returned with the required visa and permit. The flight ticket quickly followed, and I was off. I flew from Edinburgh to London where I met the UK crew in the bar at Terminal 3, then onto Jakarta for one night then the oil company chartered a flight to Matak, an island used by oil companies in the Natuna Sea. The final part of the journey was the helicopter out to the Byford Dolphin. I did not realise it at the time but I had flown to Jakarta only to get official entry into Indonesia, the fixed wing charted flight was flying back towards Malaysia!

The hotel in Jakarta was excellent and the sub-sea engineer and assistant driller asked me if I fancied going out for a look about, have something to eat and grab a few beers. None of us had ever been in Jakarta before, so we waved down a taxi outside the hotel and asked the driver to take us to a bar where we could get a few drinks and something to eat. You know that feeling when you walk into a bar and immediately think, 'we should not be in here'. The looks we were receiving in a rather dark and dingy bar made us all uncomfortable and we left rather hastily.

In the taxi heading back to the hotel the sub-sea engineer started vomiting badly all over an unhappy taxi driver. The assistant driller and I were okay, but I still reckon to this day that someone spiked his drink. He was a big guy and they must have thought if we put him out of the picture the other two will be no bother. We all agreed it was a lucky escape!

I finally made it out to the rig and started forklift truck training. This was when I found out why I had been hired. The rig mechanic, originally from Finland and living in Los Angeles, only had one eye! He had been walking through the chemical store and one of the locals on the forklift truck had not seen him, and when he reversed back on the old mechanic's blind side he hit him and almost caused a serious injury.

The Byford Dolphin was a very well ran rig and I was enjoying the trip. The deck foreman was an older German/Australian called Ernst (Ernie) Himmler. His daughter worked for British Airways and when on his time off, he and his wife used to enjoy discount family tickets with BA. Not all of his discounted flights, though, had been memorable for the right reasons. Ernie was on the BA flight that flew over a volcano in Indonesia, choking the engines and causing them to stall. Ernie did not like talking about it too much, but one time when we were chatting he revealed what happened. The 747 lost all power and was descending rapidly. People were screaming and shouting – some were writing farewell notes to their families and loved ones. Arguments were even breaking out between passengers as the aeroplane hurtled from the skies. The end to this story has been well documented but you could tell by the look on Ernie's face when he was describing the descent, how scary it had been. Luckily the flight engineer never stopped trying to restart the engines and on something like his fiftieth attempt one of the engines started again and the pilot was able to steer the plane into Jakarta airport. All of the passengers were taken to a luxury hotel and Ernie told us he had never tasted beer like it. Some of the other passengers formed a club and they meet once a year to reminisce on their experience. Old Ernie was just glad to have survived.

The rig also had a remote operated vehicle (ROV) onboard instead of divers. I did not think much about this until later on in the trip. The ROV operator was an English lad who was married to a Thai lawyer. He had invested very heavily in a business with her, supplying quarrying equipment, when she suddenly disappeared with the company accountant. Apparently, they had been scheming for quite a while and had sold everything - emptied the bank accounts and left the poor guy with nothing! To try and start again he had agreed to stay on the rig for as long as possible to try and get some money together. But I am afraid it got worse. He also had debts to settle for her as he had foolishly signed some paperwork that left him responsible. Every time we bumped into this poor fellow on the rig that is all he talked about and after a while others, and yours truly included, were tired of hearing the same thing over and over again. We started to hide from the guy. He stopped showering and his other hygiene habits were poor. He looked a terrible mess! I had never seen anyone having a mental breakdown before but I guess that this is what was happening. According to all onboard he had been on the rig for fourteen or fifteen weeks. That is a long time offshore. He was finally caught sitting in the TV room by one of the senior Dolphin personnel who witnessed him speaking to himself and picking pieces of scabs from a cut on his leg and eating it! This was the only time I am pleased to say that I ever saw anyone being taken off a rig in a straight-jacket. I never heard of or saw the guy again. But this was not going to be the only story from the oil patch of workers being burned by the lovely ladies from Thailand. A place where JCD Training would soon be conducting training.

Returning to the UK, it was time for a family holiday and just before we all departed for a fortnight in Spain, I received a phone call from a safety and training coordinator from Santa Fe in Aberdeen. Brian Ronald Edwards was transferring to Qatar in the Middle East and if he could persuade the management there to have crane operator training, would we be interested? I told him when we would be back from holiday and we would take it from there. I must have only arrived back from Spain a few days earlier when the message came through by fax from Qatar. If we were interested the job was on. It would involve eighteen days initially with more training to follow.

Chapter 9

First visit to Qatar

I had never been to the Middle East before and had never heard much about the State of Qatar. I knew it bordered Bahrain, Saudi Arabia and UAE and that it was an oil rich state, but that was about it. I arrived in August and was met at the airport by Brian Ronald Edwards who drove me to the Santa Fe land rig base camp at a place called Dukhan, about two-hours from the capital, Doha. This is where I would be staying for the duration. These work camps are just containers with air conditioning units fitted. With it being August the temperatures sometime soared to between 45 and 50 degrees. It was not the best time of the year to arrive to conduct slinger/signaller, forklift truck operator and crane operator training! Dukhan, according to the map, is a city, but there is not much there at all. I do not know about now but there was certainly nothing there in 1995 - just sand, heat and the terrible smell of either methane gas or even worse, hydrogen sulphide. Thankfully just small amounts but it certainly stank. The canteen facilities at the camp were pretty good. This was my first experience of land rigs and it was certainly different to being offshore. With it being a Muslim state, although not nearly as strict as Saudi or Kuwait, alcohol was not ready at hand to buy. There were only a certain number of government licensed premises in that era - the Gulf Sheraton, the Oasis Hotel's Chinese restaurant, the Ramada Hotel and the Doha Sheraton. Each of these places had a detective from the police force on the door as local Qatari residents were not allowed to enter. When conducting training in that heat you would certainly enjoy a few beers. It was a matter of eating, working and sleeping and boy could you sleep with being out in that heat all day - it certainly drains you. A walk on the beach at Dukhan was memorable in the evenings as the sun was going down and with the sea breeze and temperatures going down it was very relaxing.

I met the top management from Santa Fe during this trip and they must have been impressed as, even before the training had finished, they requested me to return in September. My final night of that initial trip was spent in the Gulf Sheraton Hotel, where Santa Fe had their main offices in Doha. As you can well imagine, a trip to the bar, no matter what a beer costs, was high on the agenda. The place was full of oil industry people and as they had a happy three hours promotion of two beers for the price of one, it was a lot busier than normal. I returned in September for further training courses, and this time it was suggested by a few of the Santa Fe management people that I should move here permanently and start a training centre. According to the managers my expertise was a huge requirement in Qatar. The seed was well and truly sown, but I didn't want to make any rash decisions, as there was quite a lot going on with business in other areas. One of them was Thailand.

Chapter 10

Thailand

Smedvig from Norway had bought a South East Asia company called Robray Offshore and these guys had, without doubt, mastered the art of tender assist barges, and Unocal, the big player oil company in the Gulf of Thailand, loved these barges. These tenders suited the small unmanned platforms. I picked up the contract to conduct training onboard these barges at the back end of 1995, and after working in Dukhan to then turn up in Songhkla in the south of Thailand was night and day. It was an oil town, admittedly, but also a party town. The bars were all full of oil people from different companies when they were on shore. Across from the Pavilion Hotel, where all the oil people stayed, was a row of bars. One that was owned originally by a French man had bullet holes in the ceiling - a jealous boyfriend had come looking for his Thai girlfriend one night and when she was with another man, he pulled the gun. Fortunately, he only fired warning shots through the ceiling, although still narrowly missing the French owner upstairs.

On the other side of the Pavilion Hotel was an area called the dark side. This was a row of bars especially there for the oil field people. They were never really open through the day, but boy did they rock in the evening. It was never a dull moment here and it was not long before the stories started to roll in. One that remains clear with me was about a helicopter pilot who started an affair/romance with one of the local cleaners. This must have gone on for quite a while and the local cleaner started to get jealous of the pilot's wife. This pilot must have been high up the management ladder within his company, as most pilots rotate the same as oil field personnel. This pilot had his wife and children with him in Songkhla. The cleaning lady persuaded the pilot's wife to join her for some exploring in the native countryside, which is more or less jungle, and when far away from anyone and anywhere she pulled a knife and tried to slit the poor woman's throat. After a very fierce struggle she made it back to town and survived the attack. What happened to the pilot, I have no idea, but I reckon the cleaner would be looking for a new job after finally being released from prison.

One fellow Scot who had a narrow escape was Tim Gordon. He was a single guy and certainly played the field. He was a service hand who had been working and living in Thailand for a long time. He knew the place like the back of his hand. He was out drinking with a buddy one afternoon when they decided to call it quits for a few hours rest. He asked his buddy to call round for him later just in case he fell into a deep sleep. Now Tim had a Thai live-in girlfriend and she was not pleased at the way she was being treated or the way he was living his life. She waited until Tim was fast asleep and decided to take matters into her own hands. Out with the scissors, she started to try and cut his manhood off! Now, luckily his buddy did call round for him when this was going on or it would have been game over for Tim's manhood! He required an emergency operation, 20-odd stitches and goodness knows how long in hospital, but Tim later married another Thai girl and fathered a child!

Thailand was without doubt my favourite destination during this time, with the cheap booze, great food, and great craic - and the exchange rate against the Thai baht was really strong.

I conducted training onboard T1, T4 and T7 during my time there and all were very enjoyable. There were no business class flights in those day but with being young and enjoying the adventure it never really bothered me. I would finish off one set of training, fly home then return when required.

Ensco came back into the picture around now as they had recently bought a company called Dual Offshore, who had old jack up drilling rigs. These were all re-named and this provided more work for yours truly. The Ensco 52 first hired me for a small job in Malaysia and informed me that the rig was going to the Gulf of Thailand and I would be required back when the new crew came aboard. The Ensco 57 appeared on the scene as well as it was also going to be working for Unocal in the Gulf of Thailand. This was all music to my ears!

All training in those days was organised by either the OIM onboard or the barge engineer. There were no safety officers in those days or very, very few! One barge engineer was from

61

Tyneside - very much a Sunderland FC football fan – called Henry Norton. Henry was a good age of a man then but what a character! He must have had some kind of blip in his life, as he decided to leave his wife and set up home with a Thai lady in Songkhla. He had a picture of her on his desk in his office and this is where the next story starts - like something from Beau Hunks with Laurel and Hardy! Just in case you have never seen this classic movie, Ollie drags Stan to join the French Foreign Legion when supposedly broken hearted at the end of his romance, but carries her picture with him everywhere, and when they are attacked by tribesman Ollie finds out that the chief of the tribesman has the same picture and he is also broken hearted.

A chief engineer had recently been moved to Henry's rig (Ensco 52) and this guy had also been living in Songkhla on his time off. These guys all worked twenty-eight days on and twenty-eight days off. Henry was given the job of taking the new chief engineer round the rig for familiarisation purposes. Once settled in he agreed to meet the new chief engineer in his office and have a chat on what was all happening with the rig. When Henry turned up at the engineer's office he noticed the picture on his desk and asked, "Why have you taken the picture of my girlfriend from my office?"

The chief engineer responded, "This is my picture - it is my Thai wife"!

This Thai lady had organised herself well. She was spending twenty-eight days with one partner and twenty-eight days with another when they were offshore on opposite work patterns. As the chief engineer had now been transferred, this obviously put the cat among the pigeons. It would have taken a bit of explaining that one. I'm pleased to say Henry regained his senses and returned to his native North East of England and his family. As for the chief engineer, I have no idea what happened to him but probably a divorce if he had any sense!

I was to complete many more trips to Thailand, as you will see further down the road, but next on the list was a trip back to Qatar

Chapter 11

Back to Qatar

Things became busy in Qatar with US company Occidental (well known in the UK as the operator of the Piper Alpha disaster) now assisting the Qatar General Petroleum Company extracting more and more oil and gas from their fields. Santa Fe once again contacted me and booked me to conduct training in Dukhan, but they also now had two offshore rigs in the zone, Santa Fe 127 and the 103, that required my services. They also wanted me to speak with other people in Qatar on the possibility of setting up in the country. I finished my studies for my NVQ/SVQ D32/D33 Assessor Verifier qualification in March 1996. This was a valuable qualification for a training provider and was going to serve me well over the years.

I returned to Doha in May 1996 and this was not going to be an 18-day job anymore. Santa Fe had hired a bunch of Egyptians and these guys in fairness were not oil field people. When asked what I thought about the Egyptian crew my reply was simple - 'I'm not sure who built the pyramids but one thing for sure it was not these people'.

Even basic slinging techniques were way above these guys! As for trying to attempt to train some of them to be crane operators - small mobile onshore cranes, I hasten to add – I was on a hiding to nothing.

'Instructor, assessor yes, I am, but magician, I am not' was my reply when asked how things were progressing.

Getting offshore in those days was not an easy task. It was either by the preferred method of helicopter or by boat, taking hours to finally reach your destination. My first visit was the Santa Fe 103. I remember this rig well because the rig manager had his own private cabin onboard and he kindly allowed me the use of it when offshore to conduct training. Santa Fe 127 was a different story! The rig had been rushed out of the shipyard from Sharjah, next to Dubai in the United Arab Emirates on cheap day rates to be on location. I can safely say that this was the worst oil rig I have ever had to sleep on. The 127 was fifteen years old in 1996 but looked at least three times that. Eight men to a stinking cabin, only one toilet due to the whole second floor being ripped apart to fit a sprinkler system, and the only sewer was a two-inch pipe that was practically choked all the time. There was one set of showers and they were next to toilets. The air conditioning kept breaking down and a lot of the people just grabbed mattresses and slept on the helideck! I have always had a thing about people snoring and this is possibly why. Halliburton had a service hand onboard and he must have weighed at least twenty five stones. Snore? He was like a foghorn on a ship. People from cabins further down the hallway complained about his snoring, and my remark was 'try being in the same cabin'. If you met him on a hallway what a job it was just to squeeze past him! He was in the same cabin as me and I am sure there were people hot bedding as the place constantly stank and the beds never looked cleaned or made!

The one good thing about the 127 was the Sante Fe safety and training officer, none other than Eddie McWilliams from the Thistle Platform when I first started offshore. Eddie had recently been promoted from crane operator and even in difficult circumstances Eddie got on with the job. When I first arrived I looked at him and asked 'do you not remember me from the Thistle?'

He kind of looked at me with a vacant look. He must have seen a lot of guys come and go over the years but when I mentioned his father Danny, who was still alive in 1996, and others from my crew the penny dropped. Eddie finally secured a Porto cabin (converted container) as an office and classroom with independent air-conditioning, so no more sleeping on the helideck for him, or me when onboard. It was a great place to get away from the terrible, disgusting accommodation. Eddie's rig manager stayed on the same compound as us and he used to often have the crew round for a few drinks at crew change as their flight did not leave until late at night. It was always good to catch up with the Santa Fe guys, especially Eddie.

I finished the training onboard 103 and 127 after a few visits, and when I headed back into town Santa Fe had kindly organised meetings with QGPC safety manager, Dave Jackson. Dave was a fellow scot who was on secondment from Mobil. I was also to meet with OXY health and safety manager from USA Ken Donaldson. My first meeting with Dave Jackson was productive and it was not long before I was hired to conduct crane operator training and forklift truck training. He certainly liked the idea of a purpose-built training centre being built in Doha, and said he would support it if he was still in the position with QGPC. The second meeting with Ken Donaldson at Oxy was also good.

'Can you please come back in the morning when I have more time and bring your presentations with you as I want to spend a good bit of time with you to discuss further' he asked.

I must have impressed this guy the following day as he stated, 'I've been hearing good things about you and now I have seen what you have been delivering with training - would you be interested in coming here and set up a one-stop training centre where I can send Oxy personnel?'

He wanted training for basic firefighting, helicopter underwater escape training, crane operating, forklift truck training, slinger and signaller training, and confined space entry training. There was not much in the way of training in Qatar at this time. Maersk from Denmark had a small villa they were using but not much else. Sea survival training and helicopter underwater escape training was non-existent and personnel requiring these courses had to travel to Abu Dhabi. As Maersk had their own rigs there they were more or less only interested in training their own staff and would only conduct for third parties to assist with the costs.

I did a bit of research into Qatar and some of my main questions was, 'who will build or convert a suitable building into a purpose made training centre?'

I certainly hoped I could provide the design and hopefully suitable trainers, but I was not going to spend any money in a country where, as a foreigner, I couldn't own any land or premises. This was also an Islamic state and we, as foreigners, had no rights and there would be severe consequences for stepping out of line.

This was when Ken informed me about a company out by the Industrial area called Vulture Gulf Group.

'"We at Oxy have a lot of warehousing rented from them and yards to store pipe work. How about I organise a meeting with their general manager before you go home?'

I needed to get home to discuss my plans with Judith, as this was going to be a game changer. Ken drove me out to Salwa Industrial Estate, close to the Saudi Arabia border, to meet Mike Gomes, the general manager of Vulture Gulf Group. He was quite a big guy and very charming and likeable. We sat and discussed the options for quite a while and then he had us look at a huge warehouse close to their offices.

'We could build a brick wall partition in this warehouse - use one side as a machine shop as we are presently doing - and provide you with a forty-five-metre by twenty-five-metre area.'

'Would this be enough?'

'It is certainly enough for me' I said as any forklift truck and crane operator training could be conducted outside in the yard.

'Who pays for this?' was my next question?

'Vulture Gulf will provide the shell for your proposal at their expense you provide the HUET simulator, classroom equipment, expertise and instructors that will be required' Mike explained.

This had my head buzzing. One thought that went round in my head was that I had missed out on starting something similar in Aberdeen a few years before and did not want to miss out on this. A guy I once met from Aberdeen picked my brains and started a training centre in Aberdeen, eventually selling out to a huge training provider for a vast profit.

I signed off to Mike with 'let me get home, speak with the family and I will make a decision and get back to you as soon as possible'.

Now this was before email was common-place and fax was the normal for correspondence. Ken and I never stopped talking on the way back into Doha. The idea was growing on me but how would we survive financially until the training centre was up and running. Ken once again provided the reassurance.

'I cannot guarantee you full time work, but there is a lot you can do for me here in Doha. Other companies will want your services, but remember I get first refusal'.

This was fine by me. I knew that living in Doha wouldn't be forever, and it was also closer to South East Asia – I could be in

Singapore within six hours rather that the twelve it takes from the UK. To reach Qatar from the UK you had to fly to Bahrain and catch the Gulf Air flight, or fly to Dubai then back the way to Doha as there were no direct flights. Qatar Airways were not the best airline back then compared to what they are these days. They had old 747 jumbo jets that flew to Cairo then onto Gatwick. The reason I am telling this tale was that the flight to Cairo was jam packed full of passengers, but onto London from Cairo it would be practically empty. I do not know about you but being in a large empty compartment in an old Jumbo jet where the overhead bins rattle and open of their own accord was a strange scenario. The airline was also dry. Other passengers would smuggle a few drinks onboard in lemonade bottles. I did not bother, as all that was going through my mind during those early flights was getting home and speaking with Judith, Amy and Iain on moving to Doha and starting a training centre. On one flight I decided to stretch my legs and started to wander down the plane. I could not believe my eyes. Here was this couple joining the Mile-High Club in the compartment. I had to look twice as I thought I was seeing things. Here they were in the four middle seats with their feet and lower legs sticking out in the passageway. I wonder if the crew ever knew or saw what was happening? I certainly did! Can you imagine if this had been the era we live in now with cameras on mobile phones?

I arrived home and was welcomed by the news that Judith did not ever want to emigrate to Australia or New Zealand and as this project would only be for a few years 'why not'. Both the kids were happy with the adventure as well. The decision was made, so I faxed Mike Gomes to pass on the news. After a short break I booked a flight back to Doha, only to arrive at Edinburgh airport with Judith's passport not my own. Maybe I should have taken this as an omen! British Airways allowed me to fly to London, and I stayed the night in a hotel at Heathrow to allow for my passport to be brought by courier. I then went off on my merry way with Judith's passport going the other way.

I met the two brothers who owned Vulture Gulf, Nasty Al Nasty and Saeed Bin Abdul Aziz Al Nasty. The plan was now, I thought, taking shape. The sponsorship and agreement were discussed and at this stage things all appeared to be okay. A sponsorship is required when you work in the Middle East and an agency agreement is similar to a contract, where commission is paid to the sponsor and they organise visas and other papers. They are also supposed to assist you with banking and any other associated articles like housing, to more or less allow you to concentrate on the business - the more money you made the more commission they made.

By this point Dave Jackson from QGPC had found plans from when his company had initially planned to build their own training centre. He had also sourced a quote for a HUET simulator from the UK. These were encouraging to see, especially the quote for the HUET Simulator. He stated that my request to be an approved training provider for the new QGPC lifting regulations were now in place. At that time JCD Training – I had changed the name of the business from JCD Crane Services to JCD Crane and Training Service and then JCD Training Services, although always keeping the offshore crane as our company emblem - was the only player in town approved to deliver this training. All we needed was the training centre.

I moved to Doha in March 1997, and Judith and the kids along with Suzie, our West Highland Terrier, would follow as soon as I had located a suitable house and things were up and running. I signed the sponsorship deal and the agency agreement. I already had plenty of work to keep me going in Qatar, but I still needed this training centre to be up and running quickly. I ordered the HUET from the company in the UK that had originally quoted for QGPC, and paid the deposit using my house in the UK as collateral against the loan. Meanwhile, every time I visited the site for the training centre not a thing had been done! Even when I was offshore conducting training if I ever phoned asking if work had started all I ever received back were lies and more lies! Judith and the kids travelled down in July 1997 in the middle of the hot season. But they were only to arrive and find their visas were not processed properly. This was yet another mega cock up by Vulture Gulf and did we ever receive an apology? You can guess the answer to that! I even ended up picking up the £300 bill for emergency visas!

Rather than ranting on about this period I shall jump forward in time. There were a lot of mistakes in hiring the wrong people for this project, but at the end of the day it was my shout as I hired them. One consultant who was taken on appeared at the airport with his wife and child. We found that he had been sacked from his job in UAE. Good old Ken, at Oxy, put them in a family room at Gulf Sheraton, as they were apparently homeless. After many arguments we sacked him, and I was left with the cost of flying them back to the UK. Another example of the constant problems was a wife of one of our instructors getting extremely drunk at a British Embassy function. We had been popular with the Embassy in Doha up to this point and were regularly invited for special occasions. When you depart one of these functions the Ambassador and his wife stand at the exit door and politely shake your hand. This provides the opportunity to thank them for an enjoyable evening. But on this evening, the drunk instructor's wife staggered towards the Ambassador and gave him a huge hug, declaring, 'cheerio the now Dave it was nice meeting you. Hope to see you again'. We were never invited back!

Santa Fe asked if I would be interested in visiting their land rigs in Saudi Arabia to conduct training and certifying their crane operators. I arrived in Dammam to be told that the driver was not able to take me to the site until the following day because of a sandstorm. They kindly put me in a very plush hotel. During my stay I was sitting in the restaurant watching the staff put together a sea food bonanza presentation. It was like a mountain of every kind of fish imaginable. There were many photographers and reporters there for the occasion. I noticed a family quite close to me who were enjoying a meal, but a commotion started because their little girl was wearing a tee-shirt and her arms were bare. The police were to be called and a lot of noise was being made before they came up with a solution of covering the girl's arms with two large napkins. The poor family had just been out for a quiet meal. If that was not bad enough, the next day the driver phoned to inform he was going to be further delayed as two American personnel were arriving and he wanted to take us all together rather than make two trips. He offered to fill my time waiting by taking me to see the Pakistani drug dealer who was being beheaded. The authorities apparently like westerners to see how they deal with these criminals, but only when it is a foreigner being executed. If it had been a Saudi on the chopping block no foreigners are allowed. I thanked the driver for the invitation but told him I would give it a miss and happily wait at the hotel. When I finally made it to the site I finished the first day with an Indian crane operator who spoke little English, and required an interpreter in class. I pulled out a video from my bag and informed him that I was going to show him a good training film from the UK, with safe crane operations and the dangers involved. For a laugh I added that there was a porn movie at the end of the training video for a bit further entertainment. The Indian operator shot out of the classroom, and the interpreter ran after him. After a little while both returned, and the crane operator was looking rather pale. Through the interpreter he informed me that a couple of years previously he had been working for another drilling contractor in Saudi and the rival company had handed in a porno movie for the crew to view when they finished work. He had been making his way to the cinema room at the end of his shift to view the movie when the tool pusher asked him to carry out a couple of lifts. He completed the lifts and when on his way to the cinema he discovered the building surrounded by police cars. The whole off-shift crew in the cinema room was arrested, charged and jailed for watching porn. The crane operator had a lucky escape. The rival company who provided the video tape had set the poor guys up. The penalty for their crime of watching the film was to have all nails on their feet and hands removed without any anaesthetic, and after two weeks in a hospital recovering they were deported and never to be allowed back into the Kingdom.

I finished this job and returned to Doha. Judith and the kids were getting their residency visas organised, but Judith was fuming at the villa I had chosen for us to live in. Thankfully as time passed, she started to eventually like the place. We visited a couple of banks to get an account organised after securing residency. Standard Chartered had a branch there but we did not think much of them and we ended up sitting with the manager at a bank called the Commercial Bank of Qatar. What a gentleman he was. An Indian with the perfectly trimmed moustache, immaculately dressed and trophies for cricket everywhere in the background of his office. When we told him our story of what we were doing in Qatar he was impressed, but his enthusiasm waned when we told him who our sponsors were. All he said was, 'be very careful my friends, one fine day will come along'. I replied that, 'surely as we are with Oxy, Vulture Gulf will not try any funny business?' He reiterated - 'one fine day be careful". His words worried us, but we felt safe enough with Oxy on our side.

Ken Donaldson hired me again, this time to write small pocket-size books on crane operator safety, rigger safety and forklift truck operator safety. Oxy finalised my drafts and the small books were published. This was no small project and kept me busy in the Oxy office for weeks. Ken also kindly allowed me the copyright to these and changed the covers to JCD Training. I still have these books to this day, eventually adding helicopter landing officer and confined space entry to the collection.

Finally, after months and months of waiting, the pool, classrooms, changing rooms, and jump platform were finally completed. This was December 1997 and the next argument with Vulture Gulf was about who should pay for the air-conditioning in the classrooms and the water in the pool. They finally supplied the air-conditioning units and we paid for the water. It took 22 tanker loads at a cost of £500 to fill the survival pool. However, we were finally up and running. All we needed now was customers through the door. This was going to take more time than we first thought but I was confident it would happen. To ensure I kept the money flowing, I picked up a couple of jobs for Ensco in Malaysia and Thailand. To exit Qatar once again you have to go cap in hand with your passport to your sponsor and have an exit permit granted. I was supposed to get a multiple exit visa from Vulture Gulf but, like everything else, it simply never happened. I also conducted a few scaffold courses in Doha and brought Barker down from Scotland.

'I will come down only if I am staying with you. I do not want to be stuck in a hotel' he demanded.

That was no problem. It was always good to see him and I will never forget his famous words when I met him at the airport.

'The Eagle has landed' he roared.

71

On his very first visit we decided on a visit to the seventh floor of the Gulf Sheraton - it was happy hour after all. The place, as usual, was packed with oil field expats. Judith made her way to the toilet, but as time passed, I began to wonder where she was. When she finally returned, she said 'You will never guess who I have been speaking with'.

On her way back from the toilet she had been speaking with some other oil field people we knew and one gentleman in their company had asked Judith where she came from because her accent was familiar. The man turned out to be the owner of a large chemical factory from Selkirk, Geoff Adams. He was on business in the Middle East and often met up with the other oil field people we knew – they nicknamed him Lord Selkirk. Judith had informed Geoff that her husband 'Craig is at the other end of the bar and he did all your forklift truck training at the factory in Selkirk'.

'I know who Craig is, please take me to this man' Geoff replied.

That was one night we would never forget. It's a small world when you meet someone from the Borders in the Middle East.

We started to enjoy life in Qatar for a while and we met some great people. Among them were Malcolm McRitchie and Andy Dickinson from the Dyvi Stena days. Both were working as safety consultants for Oxy on rotation from the UK. The kids had great schooling and things started to settle down... that was until the next disruption from Vulture Gulf. Neither of us were happy that our house in Scotland was being used as collateral for a business that had nothing to do with the UK. I enquired if we could get a loan and pay the bank in the UK. The thing is you are supposed to have authority from your sponsor before you can even attempt to apply for a loan. We met our friendly manager at Commercial Bank of Qatar and he said to try again at a later date, and in the meantime he would protect our accounts. He clearly stated, '... do not have Vulture Gulf group anywhere near this account. If they are allowed to sign cheques or access your account, you will end up in serious trouble'.

In Qatar and other places in the Middle East, if a local person bounces a cheque where he is the joint signature it is not the local who is held responsible but the foreigner. They can bounce a cheque or empty an account and it is you who goes to jail. It's frightening and it does happen. Fortunately for us we had the advice from the bank manager to protect us.

Saeed Bin Abdul Aziz Al Nasty was showing prospective clients around the training centre and the workshops at Salwa Industrial Estate on one occasion when I overheard him. I can honestly say that I have never met anyone so egotistical. It was megalomania at its utmost as he was bragging how he owned this and owned that, and that the training centre was his latest and greatest venture. Even the Indian office staff who worked for him detested him. One of them came up to me laughing that day and informed me, 'you know the old Cliff Drilling rig pictures in the hallway near his office?'

'Yes' I replied.

'He has only told these people visiting that he owned them as well.'

The strange thing is that I am sure he believed he owned them. Things were going to get worse at Vulture Gulf with the introduction to the company of yet another brother. The youngest of the three was called Abdullah Bin Abdul Aziz Al Nasty - or 'the goat' as we named him. He most definitely was not the brightest button in the box. He had been to Scotland and went on walkabout for a few months, somehow ending up in the USA to see a girlfriend. Apparently, she came from a wealthy banking family and when her Father found out about the romance, he brought that to a sudden end. After being introduced to 'the goat' I knew immediately that I would not get along with him either. At a meeting in Mike Gomes's office one day discussing training, he just looked at both of us and declared 'You know I shot a nigger once. You ever shot one?'

We just looked at each other. On another occasion he asked me 'why is it taking so long for the survival training to get going as Vulture Gulf have invested quite a sum of money and there is not much happening?'

I told him that 'Rome was not built in a day', and I also explained how a recent dip in oil prices had slowed down the urgency for training. It didn't register with him that I had invested heavily in the project, planned everything myself, and had flown my family over to live in Qatar. I suggested that he could 'visit QGPC higher management and ask them to make survival training mandatory for anyone going offshore'. But all I received in response was an evil look as he stormed out of the office.

Nabors Drilling had a small Jack Up drilling rig in Qatar called the Ocean Master V111. The rig manager was called Red Carter. What a character he was – he must have worked in the Middle East for a long time. Red asked me if I would visit his rig and conduct crane operator training for him. The job was straight forward enough, and while I was there the expats were having a whip round for one of the stewards. The catering crew and stewards onboard the rigs in the Persian Gulf are all from India. In this era the work rotation was two years on and one month off. Most of them did one or two trips then saved enough money to open a shop, and never return. This poor steward had returned home to find his wife and child living on the street. His agent had absconded with all the money and never paid them a penny. He had no alternative but to return to the rig for another two-year stint. The expats onboard liked the guy and organised a whip round to help - and I thought I was having a bad time with Vulture Gulf.

When we were in Doha it was not all doom and gloom. We joined the Doha St Andrews Society and some of the functions were extremely enjoyable. I always wanted to learn to recite poems by Robert Burns, and was given the privilege of reciting Address to the Haggis and Tam O Shanter at their annual Burns Supper. I learned these poems when offshore. A rig is a great place to learn and study on any subject. The address is eight verses, which is not too bad to learn, however Tam O' Shanter is a different story. At two-hundred-and-twenty-four lines it takes a long time to learn and perfect. When onboard the rig offshore in Gulf of Thailand I used to practise on the helideck. It was the perfect place, as you could roar it out without disturbing anyone. What I did not realise was that the painters were working underneath the deck. They thought I was going insane and the painting foreman reported me to the rig medic and OIM. Apparently, his words were 'Mr Craig go Ting Tong (Thai for going crazy). He shout and roar on helideck we think he maybe jump into the sea'.

Both the OIM and rig medic approached me on the helideck.
'You okay Craig?'
You can imagine the laughter when I informed them what I was actually doing! No straight jacket required.
I had another strange coincidence when offshore Qatar in the Persian Gulf. Ken Donaldson sent me to an old Cliffs Drilling jack up drilling rig (one of the ones that Saeed Bin Abdul Al Nasty thought he owned) as the cranes were not in the best of condition. Ken wanted an independent report from me. When I arrived onboard one of the cranes had broken down completely. While I was doing my inspection, I thought I knew the mechanic from somewhere. It turned out to be the old one-eyed mechanic from Dolphin Byford in Indonesia a good number of years earlier.

His drinking was now even more out of hand and the rig medic informed me that they were going to look for a replacement. At every crew change he had appeared the worse for wear with too much booze. When first onboard he had been found on his cabin floor a few times in what can only be described as taking a fit or seizure then after a few days he would be right as rain. The rig had sent him into town to be checked over and you can guess where he headed after the check-up - straight to the seventh floor at the Gulf Sheraton. He must have been a good mechanic for the company to persevere with him.

He remembered me from Byford Dolphin and told everyone on board that he had received the training courses because of an Indonesian roustabout running him over with the forklift truck, which was basically true. He had changed jobs to avoid paying tax as the Byford Dolphin eventually returned to UK waters. Cliffs eventually let him go I believe, but he was definitely one of the old school oil rig hands, for sure.

Judith used to take the kids to the pool area at the Gulf Sheraton hotel and often met other expat wives and children there. It was a great way of spending the afternoons. We were also members of the Expatriates Recreation Association (ERA) club. This was quite close to a mosque and some English kids could easily have ended up in serious trouble had they been caught. A local Qatari was paid by the government to attend to the tannoy system for the five-times-daily call to prayer. He must have thought he didn't need to keep doing this so he started sending his Filipino driver instead to press the 'play' button. The kids watched the driver arrive and enter the small mosque every few hours. He would rush back to the car and be off on his merry way. Now kids being kids thought they could play a prank on the driver. They managed to get into the tower where the tannoy system was and switched the tape to Brown Sugar by the Rolling Stones. The Filipino driver arrived as normal at the tower and presses the play button, rushes back into the car and away. For a good few minutes old Mick Jagger and company were giving everyone Brown Sugar instead of the call to prayers. I hate to think what would have happened if the kids had ever been caught.

One of my good Qatari friends was Moogrin Al-Nuami. This guy was high up in Customs - we did not know until later how high up he was - and we did not realise this until we needed a photocopier for the training centre. The prices in Doha around this time were scandalous so, I organised to have our one shipped down to Doha from our office in the UK. I called Moogrin to please keep his eye out for a box with a photocopier coming to JCD Training. He did not even call me back. Sitting in our hen house office at Vulture Gulf, Moogrin appears at the window with the photocopier in the back of his Land Cruiser. I asked how much I owed him for customs.

'Nothing' was his reply.

We used to meet Moogrin and his sons sometimes on a Friday and they would take us away into the desert. We supplied the booze and he supplied all the food. Our kids loved it as it was something different and the amount of Arabic food he used to bring would have fed an army. On one occasion we were near the sea and our daughter Amy jumped off a homemade platform only to land on broken glass. The cut was deep we were miles from anywhere. Moogrin was straight onto the phone and we drove to the nearest main road to be met by a doctor. Moogrin had organised a doctor over the phone and everything was done and dusted, the wound was cleaned and a few stitches applied, all within fifteen minutes.

One evening we were sitting at our villa with Moorgin having a good chat and a few beers. He was a little worse for wear when he decided he was going to drive home and asked for a 'beer for the road'.

'You are not frightened Moogrin' I said. 'What if you are stopped by the police?'

'All the Police in Doha are Al-Nuami, they will not bother me. We are all family. In fact, here is my card Craig if you are ever to be stopped by the police, show them my card'.

That was one business card that was not going to find its way into file thirteen. The Royal family bodyguards are all ex British Army and they shared two villas in an area not far from where we lived. They decided that two villas weren't needed and on the lower floor of one of them, they demolished all the walls and created an Irish pub. Entry was by invitation only and you had to either bring a bottle or case of beer. If you stayed until 5am one of the bodyguards would also cook you a full English breakfast. We received our invitation from another Scottish couple who we were friendly with. The pub was kept quiet for obvious reasons. The bodyguards rotated their duties, with one always staying sober to take care of any trouble. The one night we were there a Filipino who started acting the goat received the message quickly. I have never seen anyone being ejected from a bar as quickly as that for a long time. These chaps were not to be messed with. Judith was tired and wanted to leave but I was determined to go the distance for the full English. It is amazing the things you miss when you are in the Middle East and a good old bacon roll was one of them. Judith left in a taxi and I stayed the distance. The breakfast was brilliant and well worth the evening's efforts. My only problem was how do I get Judith's car back to our villa. Out with the ace card, Moogrin. I phoned him not expecting an answer, but he picked up almost immediately and I told him my predicament.

'Stay where you are, I will have a car come round and escort you home, I take it you will be okay to drive?'

Twenty minutes later two police land cruisers arrived asking for Mr Craig. They escorted me home - one in front and the other behind. Moogrin had even told them where I was going. I phoned Judith and told her to 'look out of the bedroom window you will not believe this'.

When we arrived at the entrance to the compound I turned in and the police officers flashed their lights, gave me a big wave and they were gone. What a sponsor he would have been, but I could not get rid of Vulture Gulf, and he could not intervene.

QGPC's health and safety manager Dave Jackson contacted me to inform that he was going back to his company, but the good thing here was he was not going far, only to Mobil (Ras Gas) in Qatar. He would be the HSE manager in Qatar and would be in touch soon regarding sending personnel from Ras Gas to attend survival training. He couldn't have been in his seat long when his department phoned to book three full classes for survival training! We were also informed that it was now mandatory for any personnel travelling offshore to any of their installations to have survival and HUET training. Things were finally happening. I offered Ras Gas a contract but they insisted at this stage just to invoice for the agreed price per head. At this time, I contacted the International Association Safety Survival Trainers (IASST) to become a member and after being audited at my expense, we now had this approval. It gave us a good quality assurance scheme and meant we could use their emblem on any advertising as well as on our certificates.

We were then contacted by the helicopter wing of the Qatar armed forces to have their personnel attached to the helicopter division attend HUET training. This was to be conducted in the evenings under the strict supervision of their officers and medical team. They even had an ambulance and doctor on standby should anything go wrong. Things were looking bright with training going on through the day and in the evenings. The officer in charge was impressed with my team and what we were doing. It was a great honour to be training the military in the evenings. The commanding officer stated that if any of the officers refused to take part in any of the course, I was to take his number and report it immediately. I did not really think that we would have a problem here, but we did. One pilot when starting the HUET practical exercises stated he had a very sore stomach and asked if he could try later. We wrote his number down and allowed him to shower, sit in the classroom and report to his medical officer. At the end of each nightly class we, as part of the deal supplied sandwiches, cakes, biscuits, and light refreshments. Can you imagine to our surprise when the class was finished here was the officer with the sore stomach sitting in the classroom finishing off the last of the biscuits. Sore stomach? He had eaten everything. I reported this to the superior officer and when he returned a few nights later, very sheepishly, there was no more sore stomach. The only other issue we had was a Pakistani helicopter pilot who stated that he did not need to take part in the HUET exercises as he did not fly over water. When we reported that to his superior officer it was the case of another very sheepish pilot returning to retake the course.

Judith phoned to inform me that Ken Donaldson had been sacked. His wife had contacted her to let us know they were flying back to the States. Occidental were cutting back their operations in Qatar and poor old Ken was shown the door. Worse was to come for me. Here was the guy who really gave me the idea and assistance to get this project up and running and he was going. It wasn't long before Occidental also fell out with Vulture Gulf and were terminating any business with them. They moved all of their pipe work out of the Vulture Gulf yards and emptied their warehouses. Now I know how General George Custer felt at the Battle of the Little Bighorn. Ken or Occidental this was not going to be good for us. I contacted our good bank manager about our success with business so far and to see if there was any chance of the loan we had previously discussed. He informed me that a representative would be out on Wednesday to view the training centre and would take it from there. I had all the paperwork organised and laid out for him to view in one of the classrooms. I initially showed him round the training centre and explained what we were all doing. He then made his way to his car. When I asked him about viewing the paperwork, he responded with, 'there's no need, the money will be in your bank account by Saturday.'

It was party time at the Douglas household that night. At last we could pay off the loan with Bank of Scotland and our house. We were now in the good position of playing with Qatari money not UK money.

Despite the Occidental set back I continued to grow the business. Qatar Gas were now interested in our survival and HUET course. They had over 200 workers and were going to make the training mandatory before anyone could visit any of their offshore installations. Everything was all coming together, but unfortunately Vulture Gulf were back on the war path. The eldest brother was back in town and he wanted a meeting. Now for someone who is supposed be a diplomat, this meeting was the start of the end. You will sign this new agreement, he demanded, which would give them 51 percent of the profits. JCD Training was also to come off the sign at training centre and be replaced by Vulture Gulf. His brother, the Goat, was also to be the signature on the cheque book. He also wanted me to pay everyone's wages and rent for their houses from my share of the profits. I very calmly said no. And I informed him there would be no changes to the current agreement until the contract termination date of July 1999.

I later found out from a couple of companies I did business with that Vulture Gulf were bankrupt with losing so many contracts, and they would probably be finished within the next few months. I was also told that the Goat was wanted by police as he had bounced a cheque with another Qatari company. There was no way he was getting anywhere near our cheque book, as it would have been a jail sentence for me. By this point their staff had not received any wages for over two months.

I asked Nasty al Nasty if they would consider selling me the training centre. He simply went mad at this offer.

'I will turn the training centre into a night club' he shouted.

The Goat was now becoming more and more perturbed. Whenever he was anywhere near me, he would pull his dish dash head covering over his face so he did not have to look at me.

Behind the training centre was a car breaking facility that had been once owned by a Palestinian businessman, also sponsored by Vulture Gulf. It did look like déjà vu with what was happening to me. In the finish he had to leave Qatar because they screwed him into a ninety percent share of profit. If I had agreed to any other arrangement other than the original contract, I had no doubt they would attempt to hammer me down to similar cut of the profits.

We got to the stage where lawyers became involved. The lies were now coming thick and fast from Vulture Gulf. They tried to have me thrown into jail for falsifying invoices. Thankfully, it was quite easy to prove my innocence with our training records and certificates issued. The Goat attempted to have the electricity for the training centre disconnected. Mike Gomes informed him that doing this would also cut the power to the machine shop next door. The Goat's next trick was to request the water in the survival tank be drained, but as I paid for this it would have been theft.

While this was all happening, I had applied to become the Selkirk Colonial Society Standard Bearer for 1999 at the famous Selkirk Common Riding. All of the Border towns in Scotland are famous for their Common Ridings, where battles are commemorated and boundaries are checked by mounted cavalcades. In Selkirk the 1513 Battle of Flodden is remembered with flags being cast in the town's Market Place. It was a great honour to be selected as a Standard Bearer, but how was I possibly going to get back to Selkirk for June 1999 with all these current troubles with Vulture Gulf?

The ruling royal family in Qatar is the Al-Thani family. Through a good friend it was arranged for me to have an audience with one of the Al-Thani sheikhs that he worked for. What a gentleman he was, and I was heartened by our discussion. He explained that I had indeed picked a very poor sponsor and if I were ever to shake them off by leaving Qatar and returning at a later date, he would definitely build a training centre if we were still interested. My reply was that I wished I had met him a few years earlier and that with being protected by Occidental, I had never thought in a million years that we would be in the situation we were in.

A large construction company in Doha, ran by Lebanese, who had used our services on many occasions for crane operator training, contacted me for a chat. They were good people and they knew of the problems we were having. Apparently, Vulture Gulf's treatment of us was being talked about all over Doha. On one occasion in a supermarket an elderly lady came up to us and asked to shake our hands. She said 'All ex pats know what is happening to you, your poor family, and your business. Everyone is rooting for you and we hope you all survive'.

This gave me the little boost I needed. The Lebanese company I had spoken with also wanted to build a training centre and be our sponsor. But the same problem existed - how to get rid of Vulture Gulf. The construction company was expanding its business and they wanted to know if I would travel to South Korea to look at a large two-hundred-tonne mobile crane they were interested in buying. The Korean currency had dipped, and they wanted to take advantage. They issued me an official letter requesting the crane inspection service, and I contacted the Vulture Gulf commercial agent for an exit visa. I also thought that if I could get an exit permit surely Judith and the kids can get one too. So, I requested an exit visa for them as well. I fell right into a trap here. The Vulture Gulf Agent met me at a supermarket car park near our villa and I handed over all our passports. Instead of issuing exit permits, he simply drove straight to the middle brother's office and handed over our passports. Vulture Gulf had now confiscated our passports!

The British Embassy was now involved, and a representative was sent to meet the middle brother. He refused to hand over the passports! The Embassy official informed the middle brother that the passports belong to the British Government, not the Douglas family and he should hand them over immediately.

'Not here in Qatar' came the reply. It was a stupid move by me – now we had no passports.

The British Embassy representative called me to say that the Ambassador was not happy as I was supposed to have threatened the middle brother that I would be coming back with the Ambassador to 'sort him out'. It was utter rubbish yet again. I had not spoken to any of the brothers directly for some time. I had met the Ambassador on a few occasions as he kindly visited the training centre with his son and other officials. As the HMS Invincible was coming to Doha we offered HUET training for the Ambassador and his staff who were going by helicopter to the ship, and we had been to a few Embassy functions since arriving in Qatar. The legal team we had hired also represented the British Embassy and I am certain they informed the Ambassador to keep out of this scenario - unfortunately for us he did. No court case means no money for the lawyers. Had the Ambassador phoned Vulture Gulf or met them and showed the legally binding agreement we had, it just might have changed things, but it was not to be. One thing the British Embassy did do to assist us was issue me with a second passport.

The Goat was up to his tricks again as he sent one of his lackeys to the bank to have our accounts frozen. The bank manager phoned me, saying 'One fine day Craig, you were warned'.

He also informed me that he had chased the lackey away, but he added, 'I do not know how long we can keep them away from your account'.

'If they seek a court injunction, we will have to hand over the information and freeze the accounts'.

The Goat also tried to have the water and electricity cut off from our villa but as all the bills had been paid, they refused. He also tried to have my Qatar driving licence revoked, and he contacted the Qatar tax office stating that I had not paid my taxes. This was a terrible strain on us and all we wanted to do was pack up and leave. I had had enough, the adventure was over.

There was an older Scots guy who worked for Venture Gulf. He had been in hospital for a while and contacted me for a meeting when he got out. He reckoned that he could at least get us the money for the HUET and get us home away from this terrible mess. It was getting very dirty indeed by this point. The Goat and his brothers were certainly planning something more sinister.

With Selkirk Common Riding fast approaching and no end in sight to this mess it did go through my mind to contact the Colonial Society and withdraw from being the 1999 Standard Bearer. I thankfully decided to just wait a little while longer. I read an article in the local paper about the Emir of Qatar and his fondness for horses. My mind clicked into gear, if he likes horses and I am going home to Selkirk to be the Colonial Standard Bearer, representing Qatar, and the fact that Selkirk Common Riding is the biggest gathering of horses in Europe, why do I not write to the Emir's Palace for a meeting. A few days passed by before my telephone rang. It was the Emir of Qatar's PA asking for more information on Selkirk Common Riding. I was requested to attend a meeting the following Tuesday and to bring any relevant paperwork. An official letter of invitation arrived a couple of days later. You can well imagine what Vulture Gulf thought when they heard this news. Mike Gomes, who was also getting very tired of the stand-off and working for Vulture Gulf, informed me that they did not believe I was meeting their Emir. I met Mike and showed him the letter.

'Brilliant, Craig you are going to be speaking with the one person who can end this mess' he said.

'Mike I cannot ever work with these people. We just want to leave' was my reply.

To meet the ruler, Sheikh Hamad bin Khalifa Al Thani, was a memorable experience. I told him a little of the history of the Common Riding and showed him the ribbons in the maroon of Qatar that would adorn the society flag. He was a huge man and spoke like a military officer in perfect English - Royal Military Academy Sandhurst trained, for sure.

'Will you be returning to Qatar after this fine event?' he enquired.

'Not for a while' was my reply.

'Please send any pictures to my PA. They will provide all the addresses'.

He then asked if I would like to have my photograph taken by the internal fountain at the Amiri Diwan (the Royal family offices).

There I was, dressed in full Scottish regalia, getting my picture taken in the Amiri Diwan. The thing is, I did not even mention Vulture Gulf at the meeting as I wasn't sure what good it would have done. Goodness knows what lies they would have told, and it might have caused even more problems.

With the assistance of the old Scots guy the price was agreed for the sale of the HUET. It was sold for a fraction of the proper value. As for the rest of the equipment we had purchased, all was to be left in the training centre. Judith did a great job here and sold everything at the house in practically just over a week. I sold all three cars. The only problem now was they would put my picture in the paper and anyone who had money owed had a certain amount of time to put in a claim. My only debtor was the Bank, and we had other money owed to us from training that had not been paid in full. I handed in the keys to the lovely villa we had rented. It looked strange to see the place empty. The owner was an Iranian gentleman who could have made life difficult for us, but once he heard the name Vulture Gulf he simply tore up the lease.

I met the Lebanese company again and they agreed to let me get home before travelling from the UK to view the crane in South Korea. They also assisted me in getting a new Qatar visitor's visa on my second passport. This was going to be very handy.

I spoke with the bank manager who explained that the big boss and his assistants would like to meet me. This scared me - what if they refused to allow me to leave Qatar with the loan unpaid? I met the general manager and the CEO of Commercial Bank of Qatar, and I could not believe what they were telling me. They had been monitoring the situation and were well informed of what was happening. The CEO said 'Mr Douglas, we know this Saeed Bin Abdul Aziz Al Nasty very well and his brothers - despicable people'.

'We will not stop you from leaving do not worry, as for the loan we would like to have a little chat with them about this'.

Apparently, Vulture Gulf went mad when they found out from the bank officials that I had been granted a loan without their permission. The cheque for the HUET was post-dated and made payable to the bank, as Vulture Gulf had no money, and the debt was cleared.

We spent the last night in Doha sleeping on a friend's lounge floor. We were deported from Qatar on Monday, June 7, 1999. What a relief. But I still had a trick up my sleeve. With the Common Riding all over and with a bit of money in Doha to collect I was about to use my new passport. I flew firstly to South Korea to Inspect and view the crane, then onto Doha the following week. I stayed with an old mate from the oil industry. After being kept against my will in Doha since April 1999 the last thing Vulture Gulf would expect was for me to arrive back. I had a list of all the companies who owed me money and collected the lion's share without any problems. These were not bad debts it was just an assurance to keep Vulture Gulf out of the picture. They would have nailed the lot had the money been collected before we left the country. I visited the armed forces accounts department as they owed us not a huge amount, but it was money owed. One of the officers said all the money has been paid to Vulture Gulf. I was only out of the accounts office for a few minutes when I received a message from the old Scots guy at Vulture Gulf to alert me that they knew I was in town, and to leave as soon as possible.

British Airways had by now started return flights to Doha with a very small landing in Bahrain on the return journey to collect more passengers. I was booked on a flight to leave in a few days' time but following the call I thought it best to escape quicker. A Ras Gas supervisor's wife was in charge of the ground operations in Doha, so I gave him a quick call. After explaining the situation, I asked if his wife could possibly get me onto the flight later in the evening. About 10 minutes later, he phoned back with the good news about the flight.

'Ensure you are there in plenty of time and, Craig, take care and do not come back here for a while' were his words.

My final stop was at the bank to cash all the cheques and empty the accounts. I also said my final farewell to the manager.

As Vulture Gulf knew I was in town it was rather nerve-racking going through immigration at the airport. I stayed as calm as possible and when I heard the thump, thump of the exit stamp on my passport I walked to the departures lounge with a smile like a Cheshire cat! When it was time to board the aircraft the Ras Gas supervisor's wife was there and once all passengers were safely on board, she asked me to come up front. There she was with most of the crew and a bottle of Champagne in her hand. They all clapped their hands, congratulating me on finally departing The State of Qatar in one piece. It was common knowledge what we had endured, and the Champagne was a lovely gesture. I could not help myself as the tears streamed down my cheeks. It was an emotional ending to a terrible chapter.

Writing about this time has brought back some sad memories for myself and the realisation of what I had put my family through has re-opened a few wounds. I think to myself that maybe I could have done things differently. It is now two decades on and all part of history, but if there is a crumb of comfort I can take from my time in Qatar, it's that it certainly made me a better businessman.

As for the visit to South Korea for my Lebanese friends, after receiving my report and recommendations they offered a good price for the crane. Unfortunately, the Koreans decided not to sell, and the guys ended up buying one from Europe. As for our wee dog Suzie she had to be put into quarantine for six months close to Edinburgh Airport. When I collected her, even although she had been away from Selkirk for around thirty months in total, when I parked the car near our house and let her out, she made her way straight for the door. Her own nightmare was finally over. It was as if she had never been away and lived to the ripe old age of seventeen.

Training course at Montrose from 1986, 16 class members

Thistle Platform on rig floor preparing to latch a rig tong 1987

On tow to location Dyvi Stena 1988

Helicopter Under Water Escape Training Simulator being fitted

Jump Platform Being tested for sea survival a very young Iain
to the left

Judith as a Guinea Pig when testing simulator

Successful escape from simulator after full capsize

Picture from Amiri Diwan after meeting Emir of Qatar

Happier times in Doha Judith and I before a night out

Free from Hell we had been through Selkirk Common Riding
Colonial Standard Bearer 1999

Ref: DA/99- 4210
Date: August 8, 1999.

Mr. Craig Douglas
Myrtlebank – 71 Tower Street
Selkirk – TD7 4LS
<u>Scotland</u>

Dear Mr. Douglas,

  I refer to your letter dated 22 July 1999 and enclose herewith seven pictures that were taken of yourself inside the Amiri Diwan, as you requested.

  With my best regards.

Yours sincerely,

Mohamed Fahd Al-Mana
Director of the Office of
The President of Amiri Protocol

Letter from Amiri Diwan with pictures after meeting Emir of Qatar

23 March 1999

British Embassy
Doha

Mr Craig Douglas
General Manager
JCD Training Services
PO Box 2515
Doha, Qatar

Dear Craig

1. Thank you very much, once again, for arranging for our party from the Embassy to undergo your helicopter training procedure. We were all impressed by the thorough and professional approach to our training. We learned a great deal in a short time and I am sure we were left with the confidence to survive a real life exercise should it ever happen.

2. We all wish you good luck in expanding your customer base. We feel sure that once the word gets around, you will have plenty of business.

3. Once again, our sincerest thanks on behalf of Simon, David, Peter, Guy and young Justin. We had a thoroughly enjoyable morning.

Yours sincerely

David Wright
HM Ambassador

Letter from British Embassy pity they stood back and did not do more to help

Scaffold course Barker with participants

Escravos in Nigeria having our pictures with on board security guards

Craig rigs high score

A FOOTBALL club chairman had to climb hundreds of feet to a oil rig's helipad to keep up to date with his team's promotion push.

Craig Douglas, who was working on a rig in the Persian Gulf, was desperate to find out how his beloved Selkirk were faring in their East of Scotland League matches.

He arranged for pals to text updates to his mobile phone but found out the only place he could get a signal was high up on the helipad.

And he had to spend 180 nailbiting minutes there as his team played two vital games.

The safety instructor said: "Some of the other workers saw me jumping about when we won and wondered what was going on."

It's a lot simpler for Craig, 49, today however as Selkirk play their final game. He flew home last night to watch the match in person.

PAD POWER: Craig, left, and pals on rig

With Malaysian Instructors offshore Saudi

With Diego Marradona AKA Freddie

Passports and Seamens cards I have used in my time

Iain and I in 2012 Singapore at API Exhibition and Conference

Givng my speech at API Conference

Chapter 12

Life back as an Oil Field Gypsy

I spent much of the remainder of 1999 with Judith and the kids enjoying life back in Scotland. I enjoyed the break from being involved in the oil industry for a few months as there was enough training work around factories to keep me going. Ken Wallace, the rig manager of Ensco 57, phoned Judith at the house in the spring of 2000 to enquire if I was still available for training. After everything was discussed I was back in the game and on my way to Thailand. A surprise for me when I arrived onboard was the OIM, low and behold it was James Broyles. James had been through the mill with a complete liver transplant. He had also lost quite a bit of money on the stock market and with his health insurance now practically non-existent due to the cost of all the treatment, it was back to work for James. It was great to see him again, even although it must have been difficult times for him. He remembered me well from the UK – I obviously remembered him as he gave me my first contract when I started in business. James had only recently moved to Thailand as rig manager for Ensco (he was standing in as OIM when I first met him again) and he was going to be a good contact for work and information. Once I started training onboard it was as if I had never been away. Ensco had appeared from nowhere, bought Penrod Drilling in 1993 and in 1996 purchased Dual Offshore. They were getting bigger and bigger and as I was now finished in Qatar, I was determined that JCD Training would be their preferred third party training provider. The Ensco 57 then drilled in disputed waters where the Vietnamese and Thai governments were at logger heads on who owned the rights to drill. I had hardly finished the training in Thailand when all the Thai crews were laid off and the E 57 headed to Vietnam. This was to be my first visit into Vietnam. To be very truthful, in those days, you could not wait to get back onto an aeroplane and head back to Thailand. With Vietnam being communist and memories lingering on what happened with the American War, I just did not feel comfortable. The Ensco 57 was one of the first American jack up drilling rigs to drill in Vietnam waters. Prior to that all drilling had been, since the war, done by Russians. They had a good foot hold on the oil industry in Vietnam.

Armed police guards in full uniform were stationed at hotel entrances. The uniforms looked like something from either Russia or China. The hotel rooms were basic for supposedly four-star accommodation. Vietnam was a different place from how we know it today. You could not be driven from Ho Chi Minh City – I much prefer the original name Saigon - to the oil town of Vung Tau City as it was simply too dangerous. It was down the Mekong Delta in old Russian ferries. I enjoyed the two-hour journey and it was certainly safer than the road. When in Vung Tau City it was dangerous to go out at night on your own. There would be twenty to thirty girls on motorbikes who were famous for mugging any unsuspecting foreigners, particularly oil field workers. If there was a group of three or four of you, they would not bother you, but I heard many stories of people being on their own and having their pockets emptied or watch removed. If you were stupid enough to get on the back of a bike when they promised to take you for a drink in a bar, you would likely be found later on the side of the road, naked and penniless.

Good old Santa Fe also had other rigs heading into Vietnam. The old Galveston Key and Key Gibraltar were on their way, which meant I was going to be conducting training there for a while and I had better get used to the dangers.

After finishing one visit, I was staying overnight in the Inter-Continental Hotel in Ho Chi Minh City with a tool pusher from the rig. We decided to have a walk in the evening and get something to eat and have a few drinks. Nobody really spoke any English in those days, but we managed to find a bar not too far from the hotel. We were just sitting minding our own business when uniformed police burst in the door armed to the teeth. We were ushered upstairs and felt both vulnerable and frightened. What was all this about? After about forty-five minutes we were ushered down the stairs and requested to leave. In broken English, apparently the owner had not paid off the police and they had appeared for their money. We were just in the wrong place at the wrong time.

It was around this time that one supply vessel came back into port at Vung Tau City without its Russian captain. It turned out the good captain and his crew had a scam going with the fuel onboard, but when it came time to divide up the money he refused to share the proceeds. It was a silly mistake as on the next trip, when the boat was arriving back to Vung Tau, the first mate brought the vessel in and all the crew stated to the port authorities that the captain had fallen overboard.

Another dose of justice being dispensed happened in Vung Tau City itself around this time. A Nigerian hand for one of the oil field service companies got himself into a mess. He was an unashamed pervert who bought a fourteen- or fifteen-year-old girl from her parents. A price was agreed but when it came time to pay up, he tried to do a runner with the girl. The family notified the local mafia and boy did they sort him out. He was found on the back beach in Vung Tau pegged to the sand with his ears, lips, eye lashes and nostrils removed. His stomach had also been filled with some form of oil. He survived and spent four years in and out of plastic surgery. The Viet Cong, during the war, used these tactics to slow the enemy down as the injured soldier was still alive and couldn't be ignored, and the casualty used up valuable resources such as helicopters and medics. The screaming of the injured soldier often lured other soldiers to go to his rescue, giving away their position and as a result they were more than often killed.

In between visits to Vietnam I picked up a job with the Santa Fe rig, Parameswara, offshore Balikpapan in Indonesia. It was an old rig but Total, the French oil company, liked the rig and had it on hire for years. The crew was allowed to fish at end of their shift, and a South African mechanic became prolific at fishing from the rig. He had made some good kit with weights and lines, and he caught some lovely fish. On one occasion he had to have a Filipino lad assist him pull up what they thought was a really big fish. Unfortunately, when the hooks and weights arrived at the surface there was only an empty five-litre paint tin, now full of mud and water, attached. The next problem was how to get the hooks and weights free from the tin. They tried all sorts when suddenly the old rusting tin gave way and the hooks and weights flew up at the unsuspecting pair smashing into the cheek bone of the South African mechanic. The weights fractured his cheek bone and obliterated one of his eyes. Oil Rigs are dangerous places, but can you imagine having to request an emergency helicopter for an accident caused when fishing. The mechanic was taken to Jakarta then transferred to Singapore as the Indonesians or Singaporeans did not have an eye suitable for a Caucasian.

When returning to the rig he contacted the rig medic one night as the stitches were getting itchy. The medic onboard, who was Indonesian and spoke no English, did not know what had previously happened. He shone a torch in the mechanic's false eye not realising that it was false. After some head scratching by the medic the mechanic became rather irritated, removed his eye and handed it to the medic - who then fainted! I'm pleased to say that after an operation in Australia the mechanic was finally given a perfectly fitting, and good looking, false eye. As for fishing of the rig, well that came to an abrupt end.

The Parameswara only had a small expat crew onboard, and it was alarming in those post 9/11 terror attack months in the USA that the expats onboard all received nasty messages under their cabin doors. The local Muslims were claiming they would take up arms against the 'infidel crew' onboard. This must have been alarming for the guys onboard, although a few laughed it off others took a more serious approach. I remember when I was onboard, one of the local crew members who did not like the OIM chased him round the deck with a piece of scaffold tubing. On another occasion a barge engineer was in a pre-load tank (which is full of water when the rig is on location and empty when preparing for a move) to ensure all is in good working order. He wasn't entirely popular, and someone dropped a fifty-tonne shackle into the tank, missing him by inches. During the enquiry nobody onboard claimed to know anything about the shackle being dropped. It must have fallen in by itself. On another one of my many visits to the Parameswara, there was a fire in the laundry. One of the washing machines or dryers had caught fire. Alarms sounded and the fire team, made up entirely of locals, was summoned. As the alarms wailed, nobody turned up and it was eventually one of the expats who tackled the fire himself with a hand extinguisher. When searching for the fire team, they were found dressed in their fire-fighting outfits seated in the lifeboats ready to abandon the rig.

Balikpapan, in English means plank of wood, and it turned out to be a happy hunting ground for me when it came to business. Out there I also picked up work onboard the Pride International tender barge Ile de Sein. This was when I first met rig manager Jim Sanford. Coming from America he had been working in Asia for donkey's years. I always found him to be a firm-but-fair colleague, and when I was on board Jim always allowed me to use his personal cabin. Earlier in his oil industry career Jim had managed to get himself into, what I can describe as, a typical oil industry bar brawl in Thailand. It must have been a little like Mike Tyson against Evander Holyfield as Jim's left ear had almost been bitten off. When you were talking to him your eyes were always drawn to the remains of his left ear.

I met Jim on numerous occasions over the years as the barge was sold to Mermaid Drilling from Thailand, being renamed Mermaid Tender Rig 2 (MTR2). They also bought an old tender barge that had never worked for years. It had been laying up a creek in Malaysia waiting to be scrapped but Mermaid bought the old Piranha and renamed it MTR1. The barge captain onboard the MTR2 was an English lad called Mike Bullen. He was a great guy to have in your team. Mike's wife was a Filipino girl who had previously been married to a successful American chemist. When he died, he had left his wife everything in his will, and this wasn't just a couple of dollars. Mike could easily have given up the oilfield there and then, but he didn't. The last I heard of Mike was that he had finished his career as a rig mover for Insurance companies. When a rig is to be moved, the insurance company always have a representative onboard. This is a high-profile position with a salary to match.

Unfortunately, in the oil industry wake up calls to the need for continuing to improve safety are never far away. It was around this time that a crew member was killed in the Norwegian sector of the North Sea. The mistakes that were made in the lead up to the poor bloke being crushed were all avoidable, had basic procedures been followed and JCD Training has used the scenario as a case study for many of our courses ever since. On Christmas Eve a crane operator mistakenly lowered a bundle of drill pipe, which led to the fatality. Imagine the poor family receiving this phone call on a Christmas day.

With work going on in South East Asia, particularly Vietnam, Thailand and Indonesia, Qatar was fast becoming a distant memory. It was good to hear from Stuart Meachen who I first met in Singapore when he was HSE manager with OPI and was now in the same position for a large American company called Global Industries. His enquiry was to see if JCD Training would be interested in training and certifying the crane operators on one of his barges offshore Malaysia. The only thing about this project was that there were no helicopters, and everything was by boat from Bintulu. This would take between twelve and sixteen hours of travelling. When onboard I met two Malaysian lads that were conducting basic rigging and slinging courses as they called them. These Instructors impressed me and after sitting in on one of their classes, I started to think about the future as I was starting to struggle to keep up with the workload. I approached the boss Freddie Uchin Liang (soon to be known as Freddie Maradona, because of his strong resemblance to the famous Argentina footballer). After the courses finished, we all travelled back to Bintulu together. It was a journey that I would never forget with bad weather and having to return to the barge for some reason or other around eight hours into the sailing. The total journey to shore was well over thirty hours. I spoke with Freddie in great detail, as we certainly had plenty of time on our hands, and explained how I was getting busy and would he be interested in joining me in some of my training projects in South East Asia on a sub contract, day rate basis. We exchanged all our contact details and I would now just wait until the next opportunity to firm up our new relationship.

It was then brought to my attention that Santa Fe were going to amalgamate with, or possibly buy over, Global Marine, and the new company was to be called Global Santa Fe. Santa Fe were having a bad time with fatalities on their rigs and it was looking extremely likely that they were going to lose their licence to trade in the North Sea. Amalgamating with Global Marine would eradicate this problem. With Ensco getting bigger and bigger, and now this announcement JCD Training were certainly going to be busy. The price of oil was also high, meaning the industry was in good shape.

Unfortunately, the fatalities were still happening on rigs, and the following one was in suspicious circumstances. An assistant driller fell overboard and disappeared. The accident happened at night and the weather in the North Sea had been poor, which had stopped all drilling. The diverter section of the "Blow out" preventers onboard the Glomar Adriatic 11 (soon to be renamed GSF Adriatic 11) were disconnected and safely lowered into a purpose made cart. When securing the diverter one of the holding devices would not tighten properly. The assistant driller had shouted at the roughneck on standby relatively close by for to him to throw over a 'cheater' bar to assist with the leverage required to tighten the buckle. The cheater bar, unfortunately, when thrown by the roughneck struck the assistant driller in the face and head causing him to lose his footing and fall to the base of the cart. He appeared disorientated and while attempting to stand up, had rolled over the outward edge of the cart base and slipped through a gap between the base of the cart and its main support structure. He attempted to save himself by clutching the steel work around the base but could not hold on and fell ninety feet into the stormy sea below. He was never seen alive again.

When we looked at the incident closer and after speaking with people who were directly involved, this happened in strange and unnecessary circumstances. The deceased assistant driller was apparently very much your man if you wanted a job completed in a hurry. He was not popular - maybe because of this get on and get done attitude - with fellow crew members, and he was obviously not safety minded. The lift itself should have only been carried out in day light as was the company procedure. The deceased was not properly secured by a safety harness to the structure or indeed the cart, as is required. The rig's stand-by vessel had not been informed about the lift as they would have been on hand to provide cover. The Permit to Work and Job Safety Analysis (JSA) were both in place and signed by higher management on the rig. We know the JSA was definitely in place because some four or five months later a local fishing boat thought they had found an old pair of coveralls in their nets, it was unfortunately the remains of the assistant driller, and the JSA was still inside his coverall pocket, safely inserted into a waterproof plastic pouch. It was the JSA that helped identify the remains. As I previously stated very suspicious circumstances indeed.

My next port of call was with Stuart Meachen at a shipyard in Ghana onboard the Global Industries barges, Global Comanche, Global Cheyenne and Global Navajo. These were all being prepared for work in Nigeria and the crews required some training. The barge superintendent, Phil Andrews, had many years of experience working in West Africa. This showed as the locals were frightened of him, although perhaps the acid burns on the side of his face had something to do with this. Years ago, when he was a superintendent onboard one of the OPI barges, an argument had broken out between Phil and the local deck foreman, resulting in acid being thrown at Phil's face, leaving the left side of his face badly burned. Had the acid caught him full in the face it could have been a lot worse.

Poor Stuart ended up with a terrible job when we were there. One of the barge foremen had managed to get his 18-year-old brother a job. He had no experience, and nobody knew he also had a terrible drug problem. The boy made his way into Accra one night after finishing work and bought, what can only be described as, a bad batch of illicit drugs. It must have looked like something out of an American movie when the poor guy was found dead on the toilet floor of the barge with a needle sticking in his arm. Lying next to him was empty tin foil and a bent spoon. Stuart had to deal with the authorities, and also have the body flown back to USA. The barges all left for their locations after training was completed and I left for the UK. Poor old Stuart was left in Ghana until all paperwork was processed and the body had arrived back in the USA.

I met one of Stuart's old safety officers, who I had known from Singapore, on my next trip. This was my first return to Australia since 1982. I was heading to the Ensco 56, offshore from West Australia, and can safely say to this day, that this rig had the best food I have ever had offshore. Stuart's old colleague reminded me of the story about an accident that happened in Australia a few years earlier. A supply vessel had pulled alongside a rig and when the crane operator started lowering the hook and header ball down towards the deck hands below, the header ball parted company from the wire rope connection. One of the deck hands was struck on the head. This must have been like being struck with a cannonball! We also discussed the time on a semi-submersible rig that was stacked in Darwin, in the Northern Territories. The tool pusher from the USA, who was a huge guy, liked to fish from the pontoons. Pontoons, which sit at the bottom of the rig legs, are usually submerged but due to the rig being stacked they were on the surface. He was using whole chickens as bait to try and lure the big fish. After a few that got-away, he ran out of chickens and shouted up at one of the stewards to throw down some more. The steward informed him that there were only frozen chickens left, but the tool pusher still wanted some and to throw one down. A few minutes later the steward appeared with the rock-solid chicken and threw it down, hitting the tool pusher on the head, killing him instantly. As with all deaths on the rigs there is a full investigation into the circumstances. That must have been some report.

While down that way it was a pleasant surprise to bump into Eddie McWilliams at Singapore Airport. Eddie was preparing to move to Jakarta to become the regional health, safety and training manager for Global Santa Fe (GSF). On his way to his new post he had visited an old semi-submersible that GSF owned called the Aleutian Key in West Africa. One of the marine crew onboard had an artificial leg – which unlike the rest of the world on safety grounds was acceptable in West Africa. The chap was having trouble with the leg as there appeared to be problems with the joint and the alignment of the foot. Rather than send him onshore to have his prosthetic repaired, they just sent the false leg and made him carry on working with the aid of a crutch. The leg eventually arrived back but he still wasn't happy. Eddie went to enquire what was wrong with the repairs. The crewman pulled up his coverall leg and removed his boot to show the replacement foot that had been attached to his false leg. As it was West Africa they didn't have any white feet so had just fitted a black one.

Chapter 13

2002, the year of Scaffold Courses

James Broyles had now taken his position as rig manager of the Ensco 50 and he required quite a bit of safety training. He also asked if we could organise an offshore scaffold course, or if that wasn't suitable an onshore course. I brought in Barker for this and to say he liked Thailand would have been the understatement of the century. The only thing that Barker did not like was when you walked into a bar and it was full of screaming female Thais.

'What a noise they make' he would moan, 'they are like screaming cats'.

I had never thought about this before, but he was correct. The first course conducted offshore went well, but it was decided to conduct the second course at the yard of the local manpower services provider in town. This made sense as all the local crew came from the Songhkla area.

While offshore we had been told about a suicide on the rig and James phoned to ask if I would represent him at the blessing of the rig by Buddhist monks. If there is a death on a rig in Thailand the monks are sent out from town to carry out a blessing and warn off any evil spirits. James had now moved his daughter down from the USA along with her pet dog. It had been struck by a car and James wanted to stay in town. I did not think much about it at the time but after being in a room on my knees with three monks for over three hours listening to small bells being rung and sutras being chanted, I could see why James did not want to be on the rig. The death had been from a horrific suicide. When a jack up rig is preparing to move, the cantilever deck is moved by hydraulics. This is hundreds of tonnes of metal. Crew members are positioned in different safe areas with handheld radios for communication. From the areas they can watch the package moving slowly in towards the rig. If there is any problem a crew member can radio the barge engineer and have the operation stopped. As the operation almost reaches completion the whole package will be edging towards the bulkhead of the rig. The man who committed suicide had been on watch at this part of the operation. With the package only around eighteen to twenty inches from reaching the buffers or bulkhead, he had rushed into the space and been crushed. To put this into a non-industry context, can you imagine throwing yourself under a huge road roller? Well this was similar, except vertical instead of horizontal and a hell of a lot more tonnage.

James Broyles was a great guy, but I did notice that his health was declining. He fought this liver illness with everything he had but you could see that he was an ill man. One thing I will always remember is that you never heard James complain - not once! Unfortunately, it was not long after this time in Thailand that he passed away. God bless!

Our next sojourn to Thailand was at the other end of the country in the Rayong, Settahip area for Global Santa Fe. This course was to be conducted onshore. They only wanted the one course because of the cost, meaning Barker and I were going to be put through our paces with about fourteen personnel attending. We stayed at the Banchang Palace Hotel, where one of the Santa Fe guys, originally from the Thistle Platform in the North Sea, lost his life in very strange circumstances. There were no helicopters to the rigs in this era and the crew change was by boat with a two-in-the-morning check in. To make matters worse the oil company UNOCAL breathalysed everyone. If there was any alcohol in your system, it was game over. There was a lot caught out with, what I thought was, a very unfair test. It would take six to eight hours to reach the rig and I couldn't understand why they didn't do the test once they arrived. Eric Hope had missed his crew change several times rather than face the breathalyser. On this occasion the operations manager made his way to Banchang Palace to read out the riot act and issue Eric with a final warning. When he reached the hotel, he asked reception to phone his room. There was no answer, so he made his way to the room and knocked on the door. Again, no answer. He then had the hotel open the door to see if Eric was inside. When entering the room everything appeared normal. His bag was all packed for the boat journey, but there was no Eric. The operations manager made his way out to the balcony to make sure Eric wasn't there. All he found was a half-finished drink, a packet of cigarettes and an ashtray. But when he glanced over the balcony, there was Eric on the ground below. The consensus was that he had fallen asleep while worse for wear, and when he awoke, or sleep-walked, he must have wandered in a disorientated state to the balcony and fell over the low handrail to his death.

The scaffold course went well at the onshore machine shop. Behind the site there was a small football pitch for the locals. This gave me the idea of a game against the machine shop personnel, and what a great night it turned out to be. It shows that something simple like a game of football with loads of beer and Thai food afterwards can be great for lifting spirits. What brilliant reviews we received at the completion of the Scaffold training course. We also won the football match.

An unfortunate incident onboard a drilling rig came to light at around this time. A perverted barge engineer, who was a pillar of society when at home apparently, had befriended some of the Thai crew onboard his rig. In return for sexual favours he promised them increases in pay and better job security if things were to turn quiet. When the pay packets were handed out and there was no difference to their wages, the crew complained to the management in town. This was when the whole sordid affair came to light. It transpired that after their shifts they were being cajoled into giving the engineer blow jobs in his cabin. I'm pleased to add that he was sacked, and I don't think he ever worked in the industry again. I often wonder what lies he told his wife about losing his job.

Our next scaffold course brought us back down to earth with a bang. I received a telephone call from Stuart Meachen (again) requesting we travel to Nigeria as the Global Comanche required crane operator, slinger/signaller and basic scaffold training. Stuart agreed to meet us at the Charles De Gaulle Airport in Paris as he would be flying from the USA to Lagos. Global Industries processed all our visas and paperwork. I had never been to Nigeria before but had heard many stories - and most were far from complimentary. The majority of Nigerian oil activities take place around Port Harcourt, but we were going to Escravos. I found out later that this was the Portuguese word for slaves, as it was where the Portuguese gathered their slaves during the colonial period. When we arrived in Lagos we were met by a huge security guy in a bullet proof people carrier with darkened windows. Stuart informed us many times on the journey that we had nothing to worry about as he had been there many times. We were driven to a safe house, rather than a hotel, and this place was guarded like Fort Knox. There were two large doors which opened to allow us to drive in. We were only allowed to alight the people carrier once the large doors were closed behind us. A few weeks before our arrival in Lagos, three American divers had headed into Lagos for a night out, despite being warned not to. They had been kidnapped and held for over six weeks before being released, with the ransom fully paid. They were apparently taken to London to recover as they were too weak to fly all the way to the USA. This had led to a further tightening of security.

The safe house had many armed guards, both inside and out, as well as a cook and a housekeeper. We settled down for the night after a meal and few beers - the fridge was well stocked with Nigerian Lone Star beer! Goodness knows what we were drinking as there was obviously no quality controls at the brewery - some batches tasted like a reasonable five percent lager, while others were super-strong eight- or nine percent rocket fuel. The following morning, the security guard took us for a domestic flight to Warra. It was then a short helicopter journey to the vessel. The domestic airport had military guards that were armed to the teeth. This place was not for the nervous or faint-hearted!

Once in Warra we were then ushered to a small Chevron helicopter base and from there a short journey to the Global Comanche. Tall wire fences surrounded terminal and refinery with guards everywhere. At night packs of dogs were released between the wire fences for additional security. Before security had been tightened, the locals used to scale the then smaller fences and drill into the pipes to help themselves to what they thought was oil. After a few deaths and huge problems with loss of production, Chevron turned the place into a high security prison. Barker and I shared a cabin when onboard and this was the first time offshore we were ever told to lock the door from the inside when retiring in the evening.

Training started and we were getting along fine. Stuart Meachen left for another barge and we said our goodbyes. A couple of days later there was great commotion among the crews about the arrival of a container onboard. I did not think much about it at the time. As there was no official classroom onboard, I was using one of the galleys. During a class a bunch of locals burst in singing and chanting, dragging a sheep's head behind them. Seemingly this was a great delicacy and they were marking a local festival by dragging the head around the complete barge. The crew had known the head was on its way from shore, and it was this that had caused all the commotion. I don't think it was only a sheep's head that arrived in the container as for a few nights afterwards, when Barker and I were walking round the helideck enjoying the evening sun, a strong smell of cannabis was drifting from beneath where the crew were congregating. This was also the only time I was ever offered alcohol offshore - obviously smuggled in the container as well. We were sitting in the changing room one night when one of the locals offered us a bottle of whisky for thirty dollars.

'No, but thanks all the same' came my polite reply.

'How about a bottle of Bacardi or Vodka?'

'No thanks.'

'How about a case of Becks beer then?'

'Honest pal, we are only here for a short time and it would not look good if the training Instructors were caught drinking offshore would it?'

He finally accepted this. There is a time for drinking and a time for working, this certainly was not a time for drinking. Some of the guys who were offshore for long periods at a time did take these liquor salesmen up on their offers and nobody was any the wiser, but it was not for us. Some container that turned out to be!

The security guards, when on duty, used to spend a lot of time on the helideck and one day they agreed for us to have a photograph taken with them, but not for free. To pose for the snap we had to give each a can of Coke and a Mars Bar each. I noted two of the guards had old rifles and the senior guard had a large machine gun. When I asked him why he felt the need for a machine gun he explained that the locals from time to time attempt to board the barge, so he 'blows them and their canoes out of the water before they get too close'. That certainly answered my question.

The training was nearing completion, and all was going well until the entire crew downed tools and went on strike. One of the locals on the scaffold course started to cry. He did not want to go on strike as he was enjoying learning the proper methods of erecting and dismantling scaffold. I thought the tears were a bit much, but the chap told Barker he dare not break the strike as the others would beat him to an inch of his life. The strike apparently was over nothing but a safety award. I did notice that one of the locals only wandered about the barge in civvies, not coveralls. I thought he was perhaps a trainee with Chevron, but no, it turned out he was a troublemaker who refused to work. Global Industries had tried to get him off the barge but the elders from the village were having none of it. The elders receive money from clients and in return they send personnel to learn to be crew members. Because this bad egg wouldn't do any work, he wasn't presented with a safety award, and so began the strike action. The safety award was nothing more than a £2 tee shirt.

The local workers became extremely vocal and there was some damage caused to furniture in the galley that we had been using as a classroom. The security guards were there with their rifles and sorted the galley fracas out in no time. But the ringleader, who started the strike, continued to shout and finger point. Phil Andrews was not onboard as he was on time off. The other superintendent was a different beast all together. With only recently being promoted he was not sure how to defuse the situation and rumours started to go around the barge that the security guards were getting ready to shoot the ringleader. Luckily, the situation calmed down and the new superintendent diplomatically defused the situation with everyone eventually going back to work. Before leaving the barge, we discovered that the ringleader had known Phil wasn't on board and had tested out the new superintendent. If Phil had been on board, he would have had him shot, according to the guys on board the barge.

A few years earlier a local welder, who used to go around the barge with a bowler hat on instead of a safety helmet, started a strike. He was shot, tied by the ankles with a piece of rope attached to a fast rescue boat and dragged all the way back to the beach. There wasn't much left of him by the time the fast rescue craft reached the shore, but one thing that was still intact was the bowler hat. Both Barker and I were pleased to finish that training project. It had been an experience, but the flight home was definitely a lot more enjoyable than the one going out to Lagos.

My next stop, after a good break at home, was back to Vietnam for Global Santa Fe and Ensco. It seemed like a different country from the last visit a couple of years earlier. New bars and restaurants were popping up all over the place, the front by the beach had been tidied up beyond recognition, and there were no more dangerous gangs of girls on motor bikes. By this time, it was also safe to travel from Ho Chi Minh to Vung Tau City by road, instead of the Russian ferries down the Mekong. It was about this time that the engine caught fire on one of the ferries and nearly sank. Luckily, no one was injured, but all ferry operations were suspended until new crafts were sourced and an entire replacement service was launched. Partly because of this the road was becoming busy.

The oil industry was now booming in Vung Tau City, and it was becoming increasingly difficult to get bed space on the rigs. I would often find myself being sent on shore for a few days until bed space became available. It was a nuisance but there was nothing you could do about it. It did allow for the work mode to be switched off and I could become a tourist for a few days. One bar, called the Labyrinth, used to move all the pool tables to one side on a Friday evening to accommodate the latest craze, karaoke, on a makeshift stage. All the oil field guys would congregate there for the night as it was a great laugh. One evening I was standing speaking with a Yorkshire lad, with my back to the stage when, without really thinking much about the singer behind me, the lad's eyes opened and he roared 'Craig who the bloody hell is that singing?'

I had already thought the guy had a good voice, and when I turned around to have a look it was none other than Gary Glitter. Here he was, bald-headed with a white goatee beard belting out the tunes. Gary Glitter had been a major pop star when I was a teenager, but he fell from grace rapidly after being exposed as a paedophile. He was obviously up to no good in Vietnam, and it turned out he had recently been thrown out of Cambodia. It was not too long after that night in the Labyrinth bar that he was arrested and served a jail sentence in Vietnam before being deported back to the UK, where he is now serving life for the same filthy crimes. When he was arrested on his way to a room at a good hotel in Vung Tau, the media were all over the story. Apparently, a local bar owner had been paid in the region of US$ 50,000 for reporting him to the police and the international media. The story in Vung Tau was that Gary Glitter had been paying off jail officials to allow him to go for wanders along the beach in handcuffs for his daily exercise. I don't know how true that was, but seeing a fallen superstar on stage in a bar was a big surprise.

When I was in Vietnam, I had dealings with a rig manager from GSF who I soon nicknamed, the Inspector Clouseau of the oil industry. What a crack pot this guy was. Ken Stockdale must have had something about him at one stage in his career, but by now he was well and truly gone. I don't think anyone would argue if I blamed the booze for his demise. When he first arrived in Vung Tau he requested the keys to the company vehicle from his driver so that he could drive about Vung Tau to familiarise himself with his new surroundings. Not a bad idea, but why bother when you have a driver on hand 24/7? Anyway, off he went in the vehicle and after quickly getting lost and calling for assistance, it took a search party over four hours to find him. I was offshore on a GSF rig that he was looking after, and I am pretty sure the OIM would have murdered him if he had ever got the chance. Whenever on the third floor of the rig, where the offices were, you could hear the OIM roaring down the phone at him. On one occasion he sent out a new towing bridle to the rig as part of preparations for a rig move. The only thing was he did not want to pay the company that he'd purchased the bridle from, to fit the termination socket compound for towing. That is fair enough, but he did not tell anyone on the rig about this. It was only when they were gearing up for the tow it was noticed by one of the crew that the socket had not been secured by the proper socket compound. If they had started the tow the bridle would have simply parted company from the termination socket.

Ken was eventually fired after being found sleeping in a bar one afternoon by a company representative.

One of the hotels that GSF used in that era was the Royal Hotel on the beach front. I remember this for two reasons. Behind the reception area was a wild bear that had been captured and put on show in a homemade cage. One night when I was heading to my bed, I ventured over to the cage for a closer look at the bear. The poor creature looked very miserable. I must have disturbed it in some way, and it went berserk. I swear if that bear could have escaped from that cage it would have had me for its supper. I made my way hastily to my room out of harm's way and any time I passed near the cage again I gave it a wide berth.

The other reason was that one morning when I was waiting to be taken to the local helicopter base, which is to my surprise an airport built by the Americans during the war with a long runway that is never used, I was idly watching out the window at reception. It was just another day as I sat there in my coveralls with my packed bag at my side. I had noticed the wind was getting stronger and there was a large glass advertising board inserted into a block of concrete to prevent it being blown or knocked over. Suddenly, as if in slow motion, the wind caught the glass board just as a young concierge boy opened the entrance door to the hotel. The advertising board flipped in the air and landed on top of the door, halving into two pieces. The top piece came down like a guillotine onto the young lad's arm. It almost completely severed it. He fell backwards and I have never seen blood spew from a wound in my life! Nobody came to help. A few girls who were nearby started screaming and this poor lad was lying on the floor in deep shock with blood spurting out of the wound. I admit I'm not the best when it comes to blood, and I don't possess the greatest first aid skills, but all of my survival training from through the years did kick in. I knew it was vital to stop the bleeding and get him urgent medical attention. I shouted at the reception area for someone to bring towels. Within seconds the staff were handing me a pile of towels that I used to compress the wound. The flow of blood stopped and eventually a few long minutes later an old beaten up ambulance arrived with medics. They relieved me of my first aid duties and stretchered the casualty away to hospital. When my driver arrived, I was standing covered from head to toe in blood.

Nobody spoke much English back then, and when I tried to explain that I needed to wash and change, the driver simply said, 'Urgent helicopter must go'. The receptionist handed me some paper handkerchiefs to clean myself the best I could. I still looked as though I had just come out of an operating theatre and received some strange looks when checking in at the helicopter base! When I finally arrived offshore and the OIM looked at me and quipped, 'You been in a brawl Craig?' The OIM incidentally was another blast from the past, Ash (Michael) Scrivener - the first candidate to receive full marks on a Slinger/Signaller course exam all those years ago on board a Penrod rig in the North Sea when I first started in business. I am pleased to say we still keep in touch and Ash is now an operations manager. Another success story I am pleased to say from roustabout all those years ago to the top of the tree.

One thing I realised after this incident is that there has been so much violence in Vietnam over the years, and with motor scooter accidents, this incident was only looked upon as a minor accident. As for the concierge boy, I never knew what happened to his arm. I hope they saved it. I certainly tried my best to help.

My next trip was to Singapore for GSF. They were building two large jack-up drilling rigs, the Constellation 1 and the Constellation 2. The accommodation onboard was not ready for living in, meaning it was the Orange Grove Hotel, just off Killiney Road, for sleeping with a coach journey to and from the rigs each morning and evening. The list of courses they required was extensive and it was then I decided to contact Freddie Uchin, now known as Maradona. He agreed to come over from Johor Barhu to join me for the training. This I am pleased to say was a business relationship that was to last for well over ten years.

The crews employed in the building of the Constellation 1 and Constellation 2 were North Sea Tigers from the UK, who had never been to South East Asia before. If they had been living on the rig it might not have been so messy, but with living in a hotel in the middle of Singapore it was a recipe for disaster. When work finished every night, it was party time. There were guys who went home without any wages left and guys who never went home at all - it all happened on this project in Singapore. There were even guys who married the hotel staff. One assistant driller fell madly in love with a Thai girl he had met in Singapore. The only thing was 'she' was originally a 'he'. But the assistant driller was having none of it. He was head over heels in love, and that was that. He was sitting in the tea shack one day and looked a little irritated. It turned out his lady friend needed to fly back to Thailand and wanted him to pay the fare. She apparently had a sister who was married to a wealthy Thai and in their culture many wealthy Thais often have a wife (Meea La Wang), and a girlfriend (Meea Noi), and sometimes even a 1 third mistress (Geek). The driller's girlfriend needed to get back to Thailand as her sister was appearing in court and looked like being jailed for a long time. The story went that the sister had taken enough of her husband's infidelity who was spending too much time with the Geek, never mind the Meea Noi, and she was losing face. That is a non-no in Thai culture to lose face.

The husband had come back drunk to the house one night, and after he fell asleep, she set about his manhood with a pair of scissors. According the assistant driller, the severed penis was thrown into the Tom Yam soup pot. We never found out what happened to the wife. But no surgeon on earth no matter how clever was going to rescue his manhood!

Freddie was settling into the way we conducted training and after we finished the courses, we headed back over the causeway together to meet his other instructors in Johor Barhu. We spent a few days with them going over how I wanted things conducted. Freddie was also a good scaffold instructor, which was to prove useful in the months and years ahead. But first things first, and we had to get his guys into shape. It was an advantage that they were all Malaysian, as they could easily communicate with each other and it helped with Asians on the courses that they were being taught by one of their own rather than an expat.

What we needed now was a plan on how we could execute the training. None of them could be crane instructors but they could deliver other courses such as confined space entry, forklift truck operator safety, abrasive wheels, and rigger/slinger courses. I decided on the plan where I would arrive first onboard the rig and take care of the crane operator training, before devising a schedule of the additional training and how many local instructors would be required. The plan was that they would arrive and take care of the rest of the courses, allowing me to step back and supervise that everything was delivered to standard. All the Malaysian trainers were computer literate and our training records were kept on Excel. We also introduced time sheets to ensure we knew how many days that each instructor was offshore with signatures required from both the instructor and the OIM onboard. The training records were also a good way of knowing who had attended what courses and who had delivered the course. Things were taking shape, and both Ensco and Global Santa Fe were delighted with the improved service. It also meant if I was flying down from the UK they would share the cost of my flight. The extra bonus for me was no more economy flights as it was agreed that any journey lasting over six hours would be in business class. Having the additional trainers also allowed me more time to concentrate on marketing our services and expanding our client base. It was not long before JCD Training picked up Mermaid Drilling from Thailand and KCA Deutag from the UK. We were now in the strong position of being able to cater for any size of training requirement – large or small.

I started training onboard another Ensco rig in Singapore, the Ensco 81. This rig had been brought down from the USA after being involved in a blow out in the Gulf of Mexico. The rig was brought to the Singapore shipyard for extensive repairs and upgrading. Crews from the US were also brought down. Onboard it was all rush-rush to get the rig out and start making money. A lucrative contract was waiting, the minute the upgrade and repair work was completed. I was asked at the last minute if I could put on a scaffold course. With Freddie and his guys on another project I brought down the bold Barker from Scotland. We spent the first couple of days finding Scaffold GB in Singapore to hire materials and tools for the participants. The local shipyard scaffold materials were poor quality and none of Barker's tools would match the Chinese fittings. The shipyard's own scaffolding department became curious observers while we were conducting our course. They had never seen anything like what Barker was demonstrating. It's safe to say we were miles ahead of them at the time.

With the amount of money being spent on this rig, the new galley resembled a five-star restaurant from the Hilton hotel group. But within weeks these American crews, who had never worked outside the States before, had taken the shine off the place. They all came from the deep south, Louisiana and Mississippi way, and meal-times can only be described as being like part of a chimpanzee's tea party! In they would tramp for lunch or dinner in work boots and dirty work clothes, and nobody said a word. As for table manners, well you can forget that. If anyone of importance, such as senior management, came into the galley during meal breaks, rather than show respect they just grew even louder as they began hollering out to grab attention. It didn't matter what was in their mouths, most of it came out as they hollered towards each other – it really was disgusting. Barker and I are certainly not angels, but I was delighted when he suggested we eat at another time from the newly-named 'swamp dodgers'. Thankfully, the camp boss was happy to accommodate our eating request.

There was one occasion when we noticed two of their crew watching us eat.

'Go on, you ask them' I heard one say to the other.

'Excuse me sirs' he began, 'can your children hold a fork and knife like that?'

Neither of us was sure what to make of his question, but we both replied, 'of course'.

'See, told you so' one said to the other.

It turned out they had never been shown how to properly use a knife and fork – they simply dug in with their spoon-fork contraption. It was brought to our attention that one of them was a Justice of the Peace at home, so we watched him discreetly as he ate a steak one day. His hands were filthy, there were dirty paper napkins all over the table, and he cut up the steak into small pieces with a spoon and a knife, before drenching it all in brown sauce. Once the cutting and dowsing was over it was time to start eating and talking, with bit of his steak spraying all over the shop.

I promised Barker a night out in Singapore before he would be flying back to the UK. With the scaffold course all finished, we decided to wash up and dress up for the night out. Barker headed to the toilet before meeting me on the gang way, But when he appeared, he was covered in, well, something from the toilets. There had been problems with the toilets and, without telling anyone, they purged the system. And guess who was standing next to the urinals at the time.

The laundry guy quickly washed Barker's shirt and trouser, and after another quick shower we were on our way to Orchard Road. Barker flew home the following day and I followed him back to the UK a week later. Unfortunately, he was flying home without his mobile phone. He had left his old Nokia on charge in our classroom and when we returned from our night out someone had swiped both the phone and the charger. I felt responsible as I had told him that it would be okay to leave. To make matters worse my laptop had been left and the thief hadn't bothered to touch it. You learn that anything of value on a rig will disappear unless it's nailed down.

With all the travelling I was doing around this time I needed two passports – one for travel while the other was in an embassy as part of a visa application. My first journey to East Timor came after Singapore as Ensco required training onboard the Ensco 104. East Timor is a small country that had recently broken away from Indonesia – and what a place to try and reach. I had to fly to Perth, Australia then onto Darwin. After staying the night in Darwin I caught a chartered flight with the oil company out to Dili. After passport control armed guards drove us to a helicopter base, from where we flew out to the rig. After the job was finished it was the same all the way back. On my second visit I tried to be clever and save a hell of a travelling time. Things had settled down slightly in Dili and after talking with the company man on my travel predicament, Ensco agreed to allow me to be taken by security guards to the airport and board a flight to Bali then onto Bangkok. This was going to save me something in the region of twenty-four hours. All was going to plan and I boarded the plane for Bali from Dili. A thin Arabic looking young guy with a plastic bag sat in the same row as me. I noticed he was keeping a close eye on the bag he was carrying. About thirty minutes after take-off, the pilot made an announcement that the plane had technical problems and was returning to Dili. As I was in the window seat, I could see when we arrived back that there were police and military vehicles everywhere. The Arabic guy sitting in the aisle seat put the plastic bag in the empty middle seat and I could not help noticing it was full of US dollars. The crew asked everyone to be seated and within seconds there were military officers and police arresting my neighbour.

It turned out he was a wanted terrorist and had been hiding or planning something in East Timor. He had escaped capture with a false passport but there was no way the authorities were allowing him into Bali. Once he had been taken from the plane we all had to disembark from the plane too. The suspect terrorist was put against a wall and beaten with long wooden poles. I watched the whole incident from the comfort of my seat in the departure lounge. He was then bundled into a vehicle and taken away.

All my travel plans were now in a mess as I had missed my connecting flight onto Bangkok. I was left with no option but to book a hotel and stay the night in Bali then head onto Bangkok the next day. I stayed in the area in Bali where the night club had been bombed by terrorists. The officials demolished the building and all that was left was the ground where it had once stood. It was very eerie, standing looking at the area where all those innocent people had lost their lives on that terrible night.

Bangkok was becoming a favourite haunt for me during these years. There was even a Scottish Pub on the corner of Sukhmavit 22 and it was very popular with all expats. One story that stuck with me from the Scottish bar was about an old fat German who, even although he had spent a lot of time in Thailand, was constantly being ripped off by the bar girls. He finally snapped when all his money had gone and decided to take his own life. He booked himself in to a top floor room of an old hotel in one of the ill-reputed districts. He drank a full bottle of Thai whisky, opened the window and climbed onto the ledge before throwing himself off. Thailand is very like America with no cables buried under ground - they are all untidily attached to telegraph poles. On his way down the German landed on the wires, catapulting him onto the green canopy of a nearby 7-11 grocery store. He spent months in hospital recovering from goodness knows how many broken bones. Who paid the hospital bills? I have no idea. To add salt to the wounds, when he was starting to recover the manager of the 7-11 store paid him a visit and presented him with the bill for the repair of the green canopy.

Next stop on my travels was Iran Jaya as it was once called, now known as Papua Indonesia or West Papua. Getting there was another headache! You had to fly into Singapore for a visa for Indonesia, onto Jakarta, and then another five-hour flight with Garuda Airlines. This company was not for the nervous, because of their poor safety record they were not allowed to fly into Europe. Freddie and two of his Instructors would be accompanying me on this project for the Ensco 102, which was drilling for BP who had a large compound in the area. I finally landed and was taken by Land Rover to the compound for the short boat trip to the rig. We passed a couple of Japanese WW2 aircraft on our way that had been brought down. This area was a war graveyard as there was small fencing around the wrecks. I think there was an American one as well. It didn't seem as though the world outside the fence had progressed all that much either since the end of the war – it was like stepping back in time. We arrived at the compound to be told that we would have to spend the night there as the boat would not be going to the rig until the following morning. You could just about swim out to the rig, it was that close. To add to the frustration there were no spare rooms left at the inn, meaning we were all going to bunk down together. One thing that wasn't mentioned on our arrival was the building tensions between locals and the company over money. There I was stamping my feet in the BP representative's office about the accommodation arrangements while outside the locals were throwing spears over the compound fence as warnings. The first we learned about the tensions was when we were ordered to stay indoors until negotiations had concluded.

I spent much of the evening watching the protests from the safety of my window, thinking 'what another fine mess I've gotten myself into'. To make matters worse, the air-conditioning inside the converted container was prone to breaking down every few hours. Morning came and by lunch time when we were due to go to the rig, the dispute had been settled with the locals. Apparently, the spear throwing demonstrations and chanting outside the perimeter fence was a storm in a teacup. Thankfully, there were no more issues during this trip. Once I had our trainers sorted out for delivering the courses, I grabbed the next flight back to civilisation.

My next trip was to Balikpapan, Kalimantan on the Indonesian side of Borneo. The Ensco 1 was a swamp barge drilling for the French company, Total. I was waiting for the helicopter when I noticed a familiar face in the waiting room. It was none other than Ernie 'Sizzler' Lawrence from the Dyvi Stena. He was the OIM that tried to have me sacked on more than a few occasions. I completely ignored the guy, walking away with a grin on my face.

I did a couple of trips to the Ensco 1 - on some occasions you would go by helicopter or travel by fast boat, as it was called. Helicopter was the preferred method as this place did have some dangerous locals ready to take advantage of any mishaps. The Dayak people are not just head-hunters with spears, but rumours were rife about them being cannibals. I'm pleased to say that the only time I ever did see any of the Dayak was from the air. They keep themselves pretty much to themselves and do not have much to do with civilisation. Another worry with the boats was the crocodiles, who I often saw lazing around the sides of the swamps waiting for a boat to hopefully capsize.

After completing the Ensco 1 training, it was back home for a well-earned break and to organise more projects for the Malaysian team. With the team now being able to operate without me, my next assignment was back to Australia for Ensco. What they requested this time was rather than having me fly back to the UK after finishing the first visit to the rigs, was to have a break in Australia before returning to Perth for more training before finally heading home. This was fine by me as I had not seen some old friends in Sydney for a long time. Everything was going to plan – the first courses were completed, and I had some time off in Sydney. I flew back to Perth and booked into my hotel awaiting on the check in time for scheduled flight to 'Karratha' and then onto Ensco 56 by helicopter. I was looking forward to getting the courses done and returning home after six weeks on the road. The telephone rang and I was informed that there had been a fatality on the Ensco 56. I was told to wait on standby at the hotel as the rig was shut down and the Australian Police were heading out to the rig.

The first thing that goes through your head when you hear those terrible words of a fatality is the rig floor where all the drilling operations happen. If there is going to be a fatality on a rig, nine times out of ten, even nineteen out of twenty, it is going to be the drill floor. On this occasion, however, it wasn't. The camp boss, I was informed, had been killed! To say the reasons behind his death was down to a series of unfortunate events, would be an understatement. The Ensco 56 is an old rig and when food supplies were brought onboard the rig by a supply vessel and lifted onboard by crane, the refrigerated container was simply landed on the main deck. It was a case of all hands on deck to transport the supplies up two sets of stairs to the stores area. When the rig had been in the shipyard a short time earlier, a landing area for the food containers, outside the stores area, had been created. This certainly made unloading the food containers much simpler and faster. As backup it was agreed that the crane would remain hooked onto the container to provide additional safety. On the day in question the container that arrived with groceries was a good bit longer than the normal one, and the refrigerator motor was a good deal heavier. With all the groceries safely stored away, the camp boss was inside the container with his check list, walking along the empty shelves ensuring he had everything tallied up. Meanwhile the oil company representative urgently required the crane for some important tools to be brought to the rig floor. The crane was unhooked from the container. By now the camp boss was nearing the far end of the container as he completed his checks. With the crane now no longer holding the container, the extra weight of the motor as well as the weight of the camp boss led to the container toppling over the edge. It fell from the loading area crashing on to the deck below before bouncing over the side and into the sea. At this stage nobody knew the camp boss was inside. The stand-by vessel was sent for and with the container bopping about on the sea they managed to hook the container onto the small crane and bring it onboard. The crews of both the stand-by vessel and those on the rig were all smiling and shaking their heads at the silly mistakes that allowed for the container to fall into the sea. It was only when the container was tilted onto its side on board the supply vessel deck to allow the water to drain out that the body of the camp boss floated out as well. It was later discovered that he had broken his neck. The crew, who were quite young and relatively new to the offshore industry, received counselling very quickly.

The camp boss was popular with all the lads onboard - to make matters even worse, he was sixty-five years old and on the second week of his last trip offshore before retiring! After sitting in the hotel for three or four days I was informed that the rig was going to be shut down for a considerable time for the police to conduct a full investigation. I just had to reschedule my flights and head home a bit earlier than expected. I returned to the Ensco 56 sometime later to take the remaining crane operators for training. I had stayed in touch with the rig and when I was on another trip for Ensco in South East Asia I agreed with the rig managers to return to the Ensco 56 as part of the same trip.

But, yet again, the Ensco 56 visit didn't go smoothly. On the morning I was supposed to leave, the rig manager summoned me to the radio room. He did not have enough passengers to warrant having a helicopter land, even although it was a short distance to Barrow Island. The rig was preparing for a move to its next location, and he didn't think there would be another helicopter coming for around a week. Here I was doing this rig manager a favour by certifying his crane operators following the terrible fatality, who previously only had Australian tower crane certificates and I was going to be stranded onboard for possibly a week. In the end - it was the only time I ever did this and would certainly not consider doing it again, but I paid for my own helicopter seat to get home.

It was back to West Africa for my next trip and this time it was Angola for GSF. They had two old jack up drilling rigs working offshore Cabinda for Chevron and a drill ship, offshore Luanda, for BP. For anyone who has never been to West Africa it is interesting to know about the languages. Most of the people speak their own native African tongues with the other most common language spoken in Nigeria, with it being a former British colony, is English. It's French in Ghana, the Republic of Congo, Gabon and Cote D'Ivoire (Ivory Coast). In Angola it's Portuguese, and in Equatorial Guinea it's Spanish. These are the main oil countries in West Africa.

Angola, after becoming Independent from Portugal, was a civil war zone for many years. When I arrived in late 2004 you could still see the devastation from years of conflict. The place looked like a demolition site with piles of rubble in place of buildings everywhere. I was shown a picture of the harbour area of Luanda when the country was a Portuguese colony and it was stunning. Yet here is a country rich in both oil and diamonds with very good agricultural land, and it has descended into a war zone.

Following a Chevron chartered flight to Cabinda from Luanda, It was then a helicopter ride out to the rigs who were both working side by side. The picture on our website home page is one from a classroom session onboard one of the GSF rigs offshore Cabinda. The reason for keeping this over the years was the fact that after many years of civil unrest and war after war, these people just wanted to learn, and it was a pleasure to pass on knowledge to them. One local roustabout wore a pair of North Sea yellow Wellington rubber boots with the steel cap on the toes. I found out later that the roustabout had a serious skin condition on one of his feet, and rather than go to the medic for fear of losing his job, he just kept on working. Despite the pain he must have suffered, I cannot remember ever seeing the guy limping or complaining. When eventually the medic was involved, and the boot was finally removed from his foot, gangrene had set in and he was sent onshore. His leg was amputated from the knee. With the rig management not knowing how he had contracted gangrene, they had to close the complete second floor of the rig and fumigate the place. The helicopter company also had to take their helicopter out of service and have it fumigated as well. All because the roustabout wanted to keep his job.

With Chevron being the big player in Cabinda, the Americans had a good flight arranged from Houston to Angola. The Houston Flyer was a chartered private jet that transported all the USA people on rotation back and forward. This quick flight meant that most Americans would be home before we were even back to the UK. On one occasion, an American, who had become friendly with one of the locals, was waiting on the Houston Flyer to get home. He had a few hours to spare until the aircraft was ready to depart so the local lad came and picked him up to act as a tour guide. Off they went in this beaten-up old car for a tour of Cabinda and surrounding area. On the journey the local informed the American he had built his own small house and asked his he would he like to see it.

'Why not' came the reply.

As they parked the car, the American must have begun wondering what he had let himself in for, as the new house was in the middle of a shanty town. The Angolan lad showed him a small hut built from empty milk crates with a corrugated sheet roof. This was the house the poor lad was proud of, and he declared that once he sourced more milk crates, he was going to build an extension. All that they had inside was old pallets as flooring, a couple of old torn seats and makeshift beds. Years of unrest and civil war had left vast swathes of the population living in these conditions.

Chapter 14

Oil Field Boom

By 2005 the oil fields were booming, and the number of rigs being built (especially jack up drilling rigs) and others being refurbished and upgraded in Singapore was like Henry Ford's car factory following the launch of the T4. Thousands of shipyard workers, almost all from third world countries, were working day shift and night shift. When onboard any of the rigs in any of the numerous shipyards, from a height you could see miles and miles of oil rigs at various stages of being constructed.

The first change that affected me was that the oil company, Unocal, in Thailand had now been bought over by Chevron. The second change was that Global Santa Fe was now being bought over by an emerging force in the drilling world, Transocean. This was eventually going to be bad news for me as JCD Training would find itself surplus to requirements. These were the words used when Transocean contacted me. Transocean had their own training department and did not need a third-party training provider. How major oil companies were going to recognise in-house training certificates, especially for offshore crane operators and drillers, was beyond me. Certificates of competence would be, as I found out later, handed out like something from inside a Kellogg's corn flakes packet.

The third change was that Smedvig was being bought over by a Norwegian shipping magnate and the new company was to be called Seadrill. New rigs were going to be built with older ones either sold or refurbished and upgraded. I got the call from the new company to see if I was interested in taking on the training, as JCD Training were highly rated by the guys from Smedvig. They were all moving over to Seadrill, and following the demise of opportunities with Global Santa Fe, it was music to my ears. Smedvig was originally going to be sold to Noble Drilling Corporation from the USA, but the Norwegian government had stepped in and blocked the sale. If Noble Drilling had bought Smedvig it would have meant losing millions in tax revenue for the Norwegian government. If the Norwegian shipping magnate was at the helm, they would still be in for a good return.

I do admire good businessmen, and this Norwegian shipping magnate is up there with the best of them. He had started up his oil venture with an investment of US$500 million. He bought three old jack-up drilling rigs, at knock-down prices, from Africa and had them refurbished. All three went out to work for very attractive day rates at a time when the oil field was booming. He then placed an order with the Chinese for three drill ships to be built. The deal was ten percent down and interest free loans for ten years on the balance. A similar agreement was reached with Korea for another couple of drill ships, and also with Singapore for a few more jack up drilling rigs. As soon as the drill ships and all the other rigs were completed, they were sent straight out to work on lucrative contracts with various oil companies all over the world. If this wasn't a successful enough business model, he also re-mortgaged all of the rigs and ships – and you can probably guess who owned the mortgage company.

Next on the agenda, however, was another couple of trips to West Africa and this time it was Freddie from Malaysia who was going to accompany me. This was to be one of my final trips to Angola, West Africa as the plan was for Freddie and the other instructors to deliver future courses. The best way to travel there, which I had found out on a previous trip, was to fly to Johannesburg from the UK, and then onto wherever you were going in West Africa. It also meant a night out in Sandton - a very plush area, miles away from the dangerous downtown area of Johannesburg - on the way home. From a previous visit, I knew a good steak restaurant in Sandton called the Butcher Shop. Not only did it serve up excellent steak, but they also had an impressive South African wine list. The atmosphere was also good. I informed Freddie that we would be stopping at the Butcher Shop on the way home. He could fly onto Kuala Lumpar by himself the following day, and I would head back to the UK. Training went well and when we finished, we flew back to Johannesburg, arriving a little later than first anticipated. With it getting near dusk, and after checking into the hotel, as we tried to make our way to the Butcher Shop we managed to get ourselves slightly lost. As we wandered, we passed a wild party going on and never really thought much about it at the time as we were more interested in finding the Butcher Shop. After a while, we eventually found the Butcher Shop. As I had found previously, the service, the food and the wine were all top drawer. After we finished stuffing our faces and drinking copious amounts of lovely red wine, we started to look out for another bar on our way back towards the hotel. We walked past what I thought was a night club with large signs stating Fashion Television FTV. One of the girls at the door, smiled and with an excited look on her face walked up to us and said, 'Oh, Mr Maradona, how nice to meet you'.

'Would you and your friend like to join us for drinks?' she continued.

Despite his obvious resemblance to the world-famous footballer, Freddie did not have a clue what was going on. I pulled Freddie to the side. I told him to say nothing other than 'Basa Malay' and I would do the rest of the talking. I explained to the girl that I was Diego's PA and the rest of party were sleeping as we had just arrived from Argentina. Smiling, I added that we would love to join her company for a drink.

The girl explained that she had heard Maradona was arriving in town for a soccer show and promotion event. Having started the charade I couldn't stop now, and I confirmed that the promotion show was the reason we were in South Africa – but added that Diego didn't speak much English. Freddie and I were ushered inside in by a couple of burly security guards. We were taken straight to the VIP area of the FTV production party. This had been the party we had seen and heard when we arrived at the back entrance earlier in the evening. We found ourselves standing beside the South African basketball team! Now I am only five-foot-six-inches tall and Freddie is a couple of inches shorter than I am. Both our necks were sore from constantly looking up. We must have looked like a couple of dwarves next to these guys and their partners. Just to make sure we wouldn't be found out I enquired when we arrived if anyone spoke Spanish, and thankfully nobody did. Everybody was very friendly and what a way to spend the last night of a trip before heading home. What a night we had! Freddie would just mumble something in Basa, and nobody was any the wiser. One girl asked me if Mr Maradona would be interested in taking her back to his room for US$2,000! Very sorry, I told the girl with a wide smile on my face, but I explained she would have to pay Mr Maradona, not him pay her. She stormed off, not best pleased, mumbling something about Freddie just being a 'look-alike' and him not being the real Diego. Thankfully, there were no other doubters.

Had we been completely sober when we left the Butcher Shop that night, I am not sure if I could have pulled this stunt off. Looking back, I think the loud music, dim lighting and being surrounded by the basketball players helped us get away with it. And, the fact that everyone was too polite to ask for an autograph. To this day I am not sure if we were ever shown on FTV as the camera crew certainly took a lot of close-ups of both of us. Please let me know if you ever saw Diego Maradona and his Scottish PA on Fashion Television in South Africa.

Back on home soil, I received an email from the safety officer of the Constellation 2, which was now working in Argentina. I did not know this at the time, but the home of the real Diego Maradona was soon going to be my favourite place to visit. I spoke with the rig manager to get everything organised and the next stop was Buenos Aries. I arrived on a tourist visa, and then the shipping agent processed my passport to issue a work visa. It was then just a matter of waiting for a flight to either Rio Grande or Ushuaia in the south of the country to reach the rig which was working for Total. I was informed that this could take anything from five to seven days, as I needed the work permit before the agent would book the four-hour flight. The client had booked us into a hotel in the Tucuman area of the city. Although it was supposed to be dangerous compared to other areas, it was a lovely place to stay. The American lads told us about a steak restaurant in the area called El Establo. I have never had steaks like this in my life - they were brilliant.

On my way to the shopping area, I walked past the place where the Israeli military specialists had captured Adolf Eichmann. There is a plaque on the wall of the apartment where he lived. When you see the architecture of some of the buildings in the area you would think you were in a European city. I enjoyed my time there, sitting in downtown Tucuman having a glass of wine and watching people doing the tango. I arrived in

Rio Grande a few days later and the first thing that caught my eye were the pictures of all the Argentinian pilots that were killed in the Falklands conflict of 1981. I thought better of showing my UK passport here. I knew the Constellation 2 from Singapore and a few of the senior crew were still onboard enjoying Argentina. The rig was drilling about 200 miles from the Falklands. Thankfully, the weather was not too bad, but we were warned to prepare for the cold winds and air coming up from the South Pole. I did not realise this at the time, but we were only 600 miles from the bottom of the world. I completed all the training and after being at home for a little while started to make plans to return to Constellation 2. I travelled with a proper warm jacket in my bag for landing at Rio Grande.

At this time I had accumulated a lot of Star Alliance air miles and wondered how I could use these for a flight to Buenos Aries, then onto Los Angeles before heading round to Singapore as I had a job there as well. I spoke with my travel agent and the best way to do this, using all these air miles, was Edinburgh to London, then United Airlines from Heathrow to Washington DC, then Washington DC to Buenos Aries also with United Airlines. The continuing journey would be Buenos Aries to Washington DC then onto Los Angeles, Los Angeles to Singapore, with a change of carrier to Singapore Airlines. Once I had completed the training in Singapore, I was to then fly home with Singapore Airlines to London then take the short flight up to Edinburgh.

United Airlines did not have a Business Class then so all the flights were booked in First Class, which I thought to myself, would be okay. However, with the airline being in Chapter 11, I was soon to find out that their First Class was not the best by a long chalk. The first hiccup came at London Heathrow when the flight was just about to take off and a crew member found a cigarette packet in one of the toilets. When nobody would take responsibility, the flight was aborted, and everyone taken off the flight. Apparently, the cigarette packet was to be taken away and examined. I finally landed in Washington DC and, of course, had missed my connection to Buenos Aries. I requested a hotel to freshen up and was handed a blanket and a pillow. I was not having this with being in First Class. The airline finally organised a hotel at the airport and after a good sleep and freshen up, I made my way back to the departures to be told the flight to Buenos Aries was delayed by another six hours. You would think that with flying in First Class, the airline would have contacted passengers at the hotel and informed them, but not United Airlines. I kept thinking, no wonder you are in chapter 11. I finally made it onboard their rickety old plane to find there was nothing to read, no menus and, even worse, no Champagne. Once we were on our way to Buenos Aries I rang for the stewardess. When she arrived, I could distinctly see by the dilated pupils in her eyes that she was on a drug of some kind. When I asked her if they had anything to read, she replied I have just the thing for you, returning a few minutes later with a Bible.

I finally arrived in Buenos Aries and it was back to Tucuman for the work permit process. This time when asking at hotel reception if there were any of the football teams at home, I was informed that for US$30 I could get picked up and taken to the stadium for a tour as well as see the game, then driven back to the hotel. I thought this was a great value, and an opportunity to see the famous Boca Juniors, who were at home against Velez Sarsfield. What an experience. If you think we have football hooligan problems in the UK, this is a different level, altogether. Huge nets and barriers were all around the pitch to stop rival fans getting at each other. The nets also prevent the fans firing pyrotechnic missiles at each other. As for a programme, you can forget that. They stopped selling programmes years ago due to the programme sellers being mafia orientated and regularly shooting each other. The only way to stop the problem was to stop the programmes. I enjoyed the match as it was a great standard of football. On the way there with one of the American guys from the GSF office, I explained that with it being South American football I did not expect a lot of goals. I got that completely wrong as Boca Juniors thrashed Velez Sarsfield by six goals to one. One thing I did not get wrong was being impressed by the young player on the right for Boca Juniors that night. The fans were shouting in very broken English that he was the new Maradona. The player turned out to be a young Carlos Tevez. A few years later I had my photograph taken with Tevez when I met him at Manchester City. I told him of the night I watched him playing for Boca Juniors in Buenos Aries. As soon as I mentioned Boca Juniors his eyes lit up. In broken English he informed me that Boca was his first and favourite club, and that he hoped to finish his career there.

On our way back to the hotel from the match, the driver informed us that if it had been a local derby between River Plate and Boca Juniors the trouble would have been ten times worse. He explained that the army, not just police, are brought in for these derby games.

With the work permit organised, this time my flight south was to be to the city of Ushuaia on the most southern tip of South America. It was used as a port for many of the old explorers on their way to attempting to reach the South Pole. I was picked up at the airport and then driven through the mountains of Patagonia to Rio Grande for the helicopter journey out to the rig. It was beautiful scenery and I could clearly see the attraction for so many people wanting to travel to Patagonia. It was just as well I had brought my extra warm jacket as it was very cold. By the time the helicopter arrived on the rig this was as cold as I had ever experienced. The freezing wind, coming directly from the South Pole, would literally cut you in half. Even although I started my oil career in the North Sea, I had never felt anything like this. Extra thermal jackets and balaclavas were issued to all onboard and I can assure you I didn't take mine off very often. Even the cranes had to be parked in their safety cradles when not working, as the cold froze the oil and the brakes could not hold up the boom. Prior to starting any lifting work with the cranes, the engine had to be running for a while and it was up and down only a couple of feet in and out of the safety cradle for about 10 minutes to ensure the oil was hot enough and the brakes would not fail before raising the boom up to working level. No air conditioning was required here.

From the cranes the sight of migrating Humpback whales will stay with me forever. I remember thinking that people pay a fortune to see these beautiful huge beasts in the ocean, and here I am getting paid to have the best view imaginable from the crane on board an oil rig. These are gigantic yet placid creatures, and it is beyond me why anyone could harm them.

Approaching the final few days of this visit the OIM surprised me by asking if JCD Training could also conduct a scaffold course onboard for the local crews. I explained that there would be a need for another instructor as well as scaffold materials and scaffold tools. He surprised me again by agreeing to my requests. You would imagine that sourcing UK scaffold materials in Patagonia would be difficult, but they were available and could easily be shipped out to the rig. First things first, I still had to circumnavigate the globe after finishing the training. I had courses to conduct in Singapore before heading back home for a break.

One thing is for sure, I will never ever do that journey again. I can still remember boarding the Singapore Airlines flight from LA to Singapore via the Pacific. What a difference flying with one of the best airlines in the world compared to United. It was like one minute being in a double decker bus and then switching into a Rolls Royce. But the jet lag at the other side was horrendous, and with going through the International Date Line on my way I lost a whole day through time differences. One minute it was a Thursday afternoon the next it was a Saturday - where the Friday went, I have no idea.

After the jet lag had worn off, it was now onto the Ensco office in Singapore and the shipyard for the next training assignment, before heading home. I flew home with Singapore Airlines and the journey from Singapore felt like a short jaunt compared to what I had endured over the previous weeks - and when you are heading home from a trip it is a great feeling. Once home it was time to relax and contact Barker the scaffold Instructor. When I told him where we were going, he offered to pack his case there and then. After a good break at home, and with Freddie and his guys all organised with training projects in South East Asia, Barker and I were off to Argentina.

We flew this time with the Spanish airline, Iberia. By the time we left Madrid for Buenos Aries, and after enjoying the hospitality in the BA Business Class lounges at Edinburgh, Heathrow and Madrid, I was ready for a sleep. Barker was an awful man for not keeping his reading glasses in his jacket pocket - the amount of times we would board a flight with him in the window seat and myself in the aisle, when he would announce his 'specs' were in the overhead luggage. On this occasion he decided not to bother me as I began to nod off, and I could hear him rustling about in the complimentary Business Class toilet bag. I was just settling down when I received a nudge.

'Is this mouth wash?' he asked.

Without opening my eyes, my reply was 'probably'.

Within a few seconds the sound of an exploding Hump back whale's blow hole filled the business class section of the plane.

'That's not fucking mouthwash' roared Barker.

He'd just attempted to gargle cologne.

I did not realise it at the time but these two trips to Argentina to conduct scaffold courses were going to be the last jobs we would ever do together. With Freddie and his guys taking care of all off the scaffold courses in South East Asia, it was impossible for me to justify the need to bring an instructor down from the UK when agreeing prices with clients. The basic tubes and fittings scaffold course that the two of us had developed in the southern sector of the North Sea in the 1990s, and conducted in many parts of the world, were coming to an end. The laughs we had during those years on the road together were immense.

On one occasion, amidst all of the crap going on in Qatar, Barker arrived at 6am one morning from the UK and ended up in a class two hours later. There had been a mix up with his flight and the eagle landed a day later than was planned. It did not matter to Barker, he just soldiered on. I remember on one flight he observed from the in-flight info screens that the temperature in Iraq was -27 degrees.

'I thought Iraq was a hot place?' he remarked.

Without his specs, yet again, he was reading the outside temperature of the height we were flying at.

As an indication of his popularity with our clients, wherever I am in the world, there's always someone asking after 'Barker, the scaffold instructor'.

'Just the same, just a wee bit older' is always my reply.

The course onboard Constellation 2 was another success, and before heading home we had agreed to pick up some steaks from the famous El Stablos restaurant in Buenos Aries. I had ranted on about them so much at home that my son Iain, who even at a young age had a great liking for steak, asked if I would bring some home. And bring some home I did. The problem here was that I did not realise until collecting my bags at Edinburgh

Airport that you were not allowed to bring fresh meat into the UK. A big sign informed me there was a penalty fine of up to £5,000 or 6 months in the jail. Thank goodness there were no customs searches on this occasion. I can honestly say that I did not have any idea about not being allowed to bring fresh meat into the country. The steaks went down well and I remember Iain coming home from school at lunch time and eating half for his lunch, telling me not to go anywhere near his other half, and then coming home from school at the end of the day and finishing the other half for his tea all cooked not rare but blue!

On our final visit to Argentina I mentioned to some of the guys on board the rig about what I had stupidly done with the steaks, and one of them suggested I would have been as well having a bag of cocaine in my luggage. One thing I was not going to do on this trip was bring more steaks home. On this final trip we flew with a Star Alliance ticket outward flight with the German airline, Lufthansa, via Frankfurt and the inward flight with the Brazilian carrier, Varig. I did not know this at the time but it was another airline with severe financial problems.

After the job was completed, I contacted a fellow scot, Stan Scott. Barker and I had met Stan in Bangkok a few years earlier when conducting training. I always enjoyed having a few beers with Stan and a good natter, mainly about the oil industry and football. Stan was now married and living in Brazil. As we were flying with Varig, I arranged to change our flight to see the famous Copacabana beach and, of course, have a catch up with Stan. With the flights all changed, Stan kindly booked us in to a hotel and told us he would meet us at the airport. Nothing, you would think, could possibly go wrong here.

We were out for a famous steak and a few beers on our final night in Buenos Aries when my phone rang. It was a rather bemused Stan Scott.

'Where are you? I am standing here at airport arrivals ready to meet you and you have not arrived' he announced.

I checked the email I had sent him and explained that he was twenty-four hours too early – we weren't flying until the following day.

Stan started ranting about taking a day off work to meet us, and nobody had turned up.

I repeated myself that he should check his email and that we didn't fly until the next day.

We eventually reached a plan for him to send a driver to collect us the following day.

When walking around Buenos Aries I could not believe my eyes - they had started selling prime steaks vacuumed packed and displaying a duty-free certificate to ensure you were carrying this meat legally. I checked that they could be carried into the UK, and I was unexpectedly packing another four of the best Argentina steaks into my suitcase.

We arrived at Rio de Janeiro airport to be met by a rather dodgy looking driver. His scrappy piece of paper had our names sketched onto it, but he did not speak any English. We followed him to his car and as it was getting dark could not really see where we were heading. After driving for about 45 minutes his mobile rang and he handed me the phone. It was Stan, or someone who sounded very like him, talking through a crackly poor line. I could make out a few insults and how this serves us right for not arriving yesterday. A few minutes later we arrived at the entrance to a hotel. It wouldn't have taken a genius to work out that we were not in a good area, and the hotel itself was a dump. We checked in and made our way to our rooms. After five minutes or so I called Barker and asked him what he thought about the place and the situation.

'What a shit hole. This place is certainly not safe' came his reply. 'Whoever has sent us here has certainly not done us any favours'.

We agreed to meet at the reception and, within a few minutes, had checked out. We waved down a taxi and made our way to the airport hotel. Less than an hour later we were booked into the airport hotel for the evening. At the bar we spoke to a couple of oil field hands who knew Brazil very well. They agreed that we had done the right thing by making our way back to the airport hotel as Rio can be extremely dangerous unless you are with someone who knows the place. They also stated that you always only take only enough money with you for a night out as it will not be long until you are mugged. One of them asked where we had been taken to in Rio and when I told him Aterro do Flamengo

147

(Flamengo Park) he looked at us with a surprised, alarmed expression.

'You have both been very lucky' he said. 'That is a very dangerous place in the evenings, and you could quite easily have been kidnapped, beaten up or even shot'.

I tried to call Stan Scott a few times, but the number just rang out. All of this trouble because he had not read my email correctly. He had deliberately put us in, what could have been, a very dangerous situation. When we were talking about this later between ourselves at the bar, we came to the conclusion that Stan must have dyslexia or something. One thing is for sure, I deleted his number from my phone and that was the end of that acquaintanceship. I never did see the famous Copacabana beach but at least we had survived the ordeal and still had four of the grandest Argentinian steaks in the bag.

Before I finish on Argentina, around this time marine archaeologists found a couple of German U Boats from the second world war. These had deliberately been scuppered, and one them had no crew quarters at all, meaning that it had carried something strategically valid to Argentina. My opinion, after reading books on the subject such as *Grey Wolf*, is that Adolf Hitler was certainly in Argentina after 1945 and these U Boats were his transport from Denmark or Spain to the safe refuge of South America. Now I am not a Nazi sympathiser by any meaning of the word, but you do not almost conquer the world to end up shooting yourself in a bunker in Berlin.

Ensco were in touch later that year for training courses onboard a rig they had working offshore Brunei. Freddie was on another project so one of his other guys joined me on this occasion. Laweh Iboh is originally from the same tribe as Freddie in Sarawak. It is a strange, little Islamic state that is also a former British colony. If they knew what was under Brunei and its waters all those years ago, I bet Westminster would never have allowed it to become independent. I am pretty sure everyone will know who the Sultan of Brunei is and how his wealth was built on oil. In the early days of Brunei, when first becoming an Islamic state, they allowed anyone coming over the border from Sarawak to bring four cans of beer with them. What they did not state clearly was what the maximum size the cans were. I have never seen as large cans of beer in my life. They were like ten-gallon drums.

When you checked into your hotel and the bell boy or staff member assisted you up to your room, the first thing they used to ask, was how many cans of beer did you want. There was never much to do in Brunei, so it was usually just something to eat, order a few beers from staff and settle down in front of the TV in your room before being picked up in the morning for helicopter out to the rig. On one occasion the Sultan of Brunei booked Michael Jackson to come and play a concert for his son's birthday celebrations. What the total cost of this would be is astronomical, anyone's guess but money was never an issue in Brunei. My passion for football goes back to when I was a very young lad. In later years I became very friendly with the now deceased Life President of Manchester City FC, Bernard Halford. Bernard was the main instigator and organiser in bringing huge acts to City's old ground of Maine Road in the summer months. Acts like David Bowie and Queen were all booked by Bernard. Bernard managed to get the phone number for Michael Jackson's agent around this time. For him to play on his own at Maine Road, the agent wanted £1,000,000 plus expenses. That was the end of that enquiry. The Sultan however, not only booked Jackson, he also booked the whole entourage and all the props. And when the concert was finished, he paid for all the props to remain in the country as a reminder of the concert.

It would likely be small change for someone who has a swimming pool in his private 747 jet. With the Sultan being a huge polo player and fan, he has his polo horses all housed in air-conditioned stables. Talking of 747s the Sultan's brother was well known for bringing a 747 full of 'ladies of the night' into Brunei. The flight would land at the far end of the runway and a fleet of limousines would then chauffeur the ladies away to his palace. They never came anywhere near the Immigration hall. This used to happen on quite a regular basis and, if my memory serves me correctly, one girl wrote her story about the time she was one of the girls on a trip to Brunei. She described how she was never picked to be a companion but still left the country with a very healthy pay cheque.

Back home, Judith's mother's health had been poor with fighting cancer. For a period of time she appeared to be in remission, but it returned with a vengeance. We spoke with the consultant in Edinburgh about the business trip I was about to take and he believed that there was nothing to worry about, as he did not expect any further deterioration for at least four months. I expected to reach Brunei, carry out the training, and return to be with my wife during her mother's final months. How wrong I turned out to be! I was only away for four days when I received the phone call from Judith that her mother had passed away. I spoke with Danny Haynes, the Ensco OIM, who I had fortunately known for years from the North Sea. We both talked with Laweh on the situation, and he very kindly told me to make my way home and he would conduct all the training on his own. I have always been grateful to Laweh for this kind gesture as had it been any other Malaysian instructor, they would have wanted to leave the rig with me. I had learned from previous experience that most of these people will not, and cannot, think for themselves. When it comes to planning the training they just appeared to be lost. They were great when it was a classroom of locals but if there was an expat sitting in, they used to be on edge and become very nervous. Thankfully Laweh was a different kettle of fish.

With everything all agreed with Danny and Laweh, I contacted my travel agent and flew home at the cost of £3,000. I was thinking in the back of my mind that my insurance would not be a problem here for such an unlikely and sad event. How wrong I was here. After many letters back and forth to the insurance company, their final stance was that as it was a known illness and they would not pay out for my flight home.

Ensco also had three rigs working in Saudi Arabia at this point, and the amount of training that was required, even with a full four-man team, was going to take more than the one trip. We worked out that to put all crews through the courses would take four visits for the four of us. With visas organised we all met in Dubai before flying onto Bahrain the following day. We were met by the Ensco agent's driver at Bahrain Airport then taken over the causeway to Saudi immigration. A stay in the Al Khobar hotel was required until offshore passes were granted. On one occasion, one of Freddie's Instructors had to wait at the hotel for ten days before receiving his offshore pass. Luckily the longest I had to wait was a couple of days.

One of the training courses on top of the list for this project was offshore helicopter landing officer and offshore helicopter crew member courses. This was 2006 and the helicopter landing procedures that Saudi Aramco, who were the biggest oil company in the world at the time, had in place were simply non-existent. None of the Saudi Aramco platforms had helicopter landing officers. The helicopters used to land on a platform and the passengers would just disembark themselves and head to the luggage hold with usually nothing but flip-flops or sandals on their feet and sunglasses and baseball caps balanced on their heads, and grab their belongings, which were normally packed in supermarket carrier bags. This was a recipe for a disaster. If any plastic bag or pair of sunglasses or cap got caught in the rotors, or worse the helicopter engines, a serious accident was likely. The passengers would then wave farewell to the pilots before closing the doors themselves and heading for the heli waiting room. I could not believe my eyes.

Once onboard the Ensco rigs it quickly became clear that we had our work cut out to bring about changes through our training. Saudi Aramco had started a policy of sending out local workers from poor families to learn about becoming oil industry hands. The problem with these workers is that they didn't want to be offshore in the first place and at every opportunity they would disappear from our classroom. The favourite excuse for avoiding classes was prayer time. Once they left the classroom for prayer, you could guarantee they would not return for at least two hours. It was their country and their religion, so there was little we could do or say. Once we started demonstrating the correct procedures for baggage handling from helicopters, murmurs between the workers grew louder. Eventually we managed to establish that they didn't approve, as they were Saudi nationals and they shouldn't be expected to carry an Indian's bag to or from the helicopter.

Eventually I got all of the offshore crane operators trained and certified. All the other training plans for Freddie and his guys to follow were also in place. After four trips to the Kingdom it was time for me to depart, leaving Freddie and his Instructors to complete the rest of the training. The project lasted a while longer than first anticipated. On my way to the airport, the Saudi Aramco HSE manager contacted me and requested a meeting before I left. He wanted to know if it was possible for JCD Training to conduct courses on the land rigs. It turned out to be quite a meeting this one. They wanted us to supply two instructors as well as a Chinese speaking translator. Saudi Aramco had more than twenty land rigs working in the desert. All of them were Chinese owned and all had Chinese crews. The HSE manager also emphasised that they wanted the instructors and translator to stay for up to six months and complete all the training as part of the one trip. I waited until Freddie and his guys finished with Ensco and were at home before informing them of this desert job with the Chinese land rigs. We agreed to hold a meeting in Malaysia on my next trip to South East Asia so that we could put a plan together. I was due to head for Vietnam and could travel via Malaysia. We interviewed a few Malaysian guys who could speak both Chinese and Cantonese. But trying to get two of Freddie's guys to go for up to six months was turning into a bit of a problem. As is normal, when you start talking money and offer a good bonus, things changed, and they all wanted to go! This was a relief because I certainly was not going!

With the training courses organised, terms and conditions put in place, a starting date agreed and the visas and flights sorted, it was all systems go. In fairness, the Malaysian boys did a good job here in horrendous conditions. They were sleeping in converted containers, which is normal for land rigs, but the air conditioning was prone to breaking down. The food sounded terrible, and the drilling rigs were old and in terrible condition. There was also an initial problem with the translator as he had a different accent from what the workers were used to. It was described to me as being like someone from Devon in South of England and someone from Peterhead in the North East of Scotland trying to understand each other.

It also came to light during the training, of how the Chinese recruited their crews. The contractor would take a bus around prisons and they would pick up convicts on their last day of captivity. These ex-prisoners would often have nowhere else to go. The rotations were nothing like what we knew. They would spend a whole year on a rig before being allowed home with their pay, and they would never return. The instructors assured me they did not mix with any of the crews and I couldn't blame them. For all you knew, you could be standing next to a murderer. We completed all the training in just over five months and the guys were glad to get home. Judith looked after accounts and the administration side of things in the office, and she still reminds me the nightmare of a job she had printing all the Chinese names on the certificates that were eventually sent to Saudi, all 450 of them!

China became a feature around this time as we received an enquiry from a company based there about basic slinger/signaller training. Having just completed this Saudi contract successfully, I admit my guard was down. This Chinese company phoned our office in Scotland on numerous occasions. They claimed that they had won a contract to supply men to a huge construction site and their people required adequate safety training. Alarm bells should have been ringing in my head when they started talking about sending their workers to the UK for the training. They claimed that around 120 workers would need certified. I contacted Freddie in Malaysia and he was confident of finding a suitable training venue with crane hire, slings and articles for lifting, and a coach for airport and training site shuttles. He could also find someone to provide Chinese food, accommodation at a reasonable hotel, and a translator. This was looking lucrative for us, and after many emails back and forward a contract was agreed in principal. A three-day course for twenty people at a time was agreed. The company even sent me a letter of invitation for a visa to visit them in China. Another warning should have been registered when they refused to meet me in Singapore.

I had business to attend to in Singapore and after collecting my Chinese visa in Edinburgh I flew onto China to be met at the airport by one of their representatives. Before flying to China, I had been talking with a South African businessman who did a lot of heavy plant sales business in China. He offered to be just a phone call away if I was unsure of anything.

Photographs were taken of myself signing the contract with their chief executive and operations accounts manager. During the meeting I was informed that I should buy their chief executive a gift to seal the contract, as is tradition in China. I was also informed that he wanted a gold ring. I phoned my South African contact and he confirmed that this was normal. He added that a cheap gold ring was not bad as he had recently been stung for two Burberry sports jackets to secure a contract.

The accounts manager then claimed that I would need to pay my share of the costs for the company buying foreign currency to enter into the contract. It worked out at half of 2.5 percent of the contract's value. Back on the phone to my South African contact, and apparently this was also normal in China. I phoned home to Scotland and the money was then transferred to their account. When the money arrived, they sent names and copies of passports for the first workers to be enrolled onto the course. The agreement was that they would pay for each class ten days in advance of it starting.

Needless to say we never heard from these people again - it was all a scam. Fraud would probably be a better word to describe how they went about things. All the above to steal a couple of thousand pounds and a gold ring. In hindsight I was perhaps lucky to get away with losing what I did. When I first met them at their office, I was asked what my position was at JCD Training. I still remember the look of surprise on their faces when I said I was the owner. It made me think I was perhaps lucky to get out with only being fleeced for a couple of thousand when I could have possible been held for ransom.

Petro Vietnam Drilling (PVD) had a training centre in Vung Tua City, which was originally started by the Russian firm Vietsovpetro. It was a facility that was seriously required in their country and when the opportunity arose, I was delighted to meet with them and discuss offshore crane operator courses as well as other lifting courses. They had learned of JCD Training from the work we had done with other drilling contractors like Ensco and GSF in Vietnam. A deal was struck, and plans put in place to start offering our services. The first visit didn't go to plan, though, as Vung Tau City had been hit by a typhoon and the place looked like a demolition site. Trees had been uprooted in the street, buildings had their roofs torn off, and there was no electric power as all the lines were down. Some of the bigger buildings had emergency generators as back-up, but it wasn't an ideal setting for launching our new courses. When walking along the street there was an awful smell of rotten meat, expecting it to be food that had gone off. But I was informed the smell was bodies that had not yet been retrieved from beneath fallen trees and collapsed buildings. With the place in a state of emergency the last thing PVD required was someone conducting a training course, and after a couple of days I flew back to Thailand to conduct final training for GSF before they finally changed everything over to Transocean.

In Thailand, one of the tool pushers onboard had recently divorced his Thai wife in what were comical circumstances. This chap had paid for a piece of land before having a beautiful house built for him and his new wife. As is the law in Thailand, everything was in his wife's name. The problems began when she asked if he minded her brother moving in while her husband was offshore, so that he could do odd jobs that were required. It emerged some time later that the brother was in fact her Thai husband. I am not sure what first raised his suspicions, but the tool pusher did a good bit of spying and detective work to establish the facts. He waited until his wife and her other husband were out of the house for the day when he went to the local police station to announce he was selling the property and he didn't need any of the furniture or belongings – and they could help themselves to anything they liked. Within minutes the patrol cars were outside the house with officers loading up electrical equipment, items of furniture and anything else of value.

Once the police had gone, a hired excavator arrived with instructions to flatten the house. The tool pusher waited patiently in his car for his wife and her other husband to arrive back at the property. You can imagine the look of shock on the Thai wife's face when returning. From what I was told, the tool pusher calmly walked up to her and her 'brother'.

He said: 'you might have cost me a quite a bit of money, but you now have nothing'.

He then calmly walked away and never set eyes on her again.

With GSF now part of the Transocean Empire, and JCD Training deemed surplus to requirements, it was great news for me that Seadrill were now very much in the picture. They were building new rigs and new drill ships as well as having recently acquired all the Smedvig tender barges that were making a lot of money. They had also started building new tender barges that were of a brilliant fully semi-submersible design. The old tender barges used to take anything from ten to fourteen days to rig up once on location, depending on weather. But these new beauties could be ready within forty-eight hours. There were two cranes onboard as normal but the larger one had an increased lifting capacity in the region of two-hundred-and-fifty tonnes and a smaller crane was to be used for everyday lifts with a lifting capacity of forty to fifty tonnes. As well as being a reputable company, the people that Seadrill hired were great people to be associated with. When you were onboard they were fully supportive of all courses as they knew the benefits from good training. The Norwegian shipping magnate that started this company certainly knew what he was doing.

A brilliant story from this era was when the company's founder and his family lived in London. They stayed in a beautiful house in Bellevue. The Chelsea FC owner and famous Russian billionaire, Roman Abramovich, admired the property, which reputedly has a Garden only slightly smaller than Buckingham Palace, and walked up to the front door one day offering £150 million in cash. The story goes that he was sent packing with his tail between his legs. I'm not sure what the Norwegian is for 'not for sale' but that was the response.

Chapter 15

Illness and health issues finally catch up

With visiting many countries in South East Asia and other parts of the world, I always ensured that I had the proper vaccinations which were recommended for the different countries. My luck was about to run out when it came to health. The first time I became ill was in Thailand. It felt as though I had the flu - one minute roasting hot, the next freezing cold – with the added misery of a really bad hangover thrown in. I tested negative for Malaria and after other tests it was diagnosed that I had the dreaded dengue fever. From all the mosquito bites I'd had over the years, I suppose it was inevitable.

This knocked me for six and I did not start to feel better for a few weeks. I had just recovered from this nasty virus when I was down in Indonesia. I was travelling back on shore by boat from an Ensco rig when I noticed something white, like a long insect, flash past in front of me. This was on the jetty at the port, and I didn't think anything of it at the time. Within a short space of time I became very ill again. This time the feeling was even worse than the dengue fever. I did not feel like eating or drinking, and despite trying to battle on I simply did not have any strength. I was onboard an old KCA Deutag barge, sharing a cabin with a night tool pusher, when my stomach suddenly erupted. Thank goodness he was working when everything just came away from me. All I wanted to do was either sit on a toilet or sleep.

My initial thought was that the dengue fever had returned, but this feeling was even worse than the first fever. Thank goodness I knew the offshore crane operators onboard and as this was a simple re-certification project, as soon as the job was completed, I made my way onshore. How I ever managed to finish this course still baffles me. I headed straight to a hotel to see if a bit comfort would help ease the symptoms. I still didn't want to eat anything, and all I felt like doing was sleeping. After a couple of days I decided to try and get myself home. I managed to sleep all the way back on the flight. Once I was back in Selkirk it was time to see a doctor. This turned out to be a lot more serious than just popping a few paracetamols. None of the local doctors could work out what was wrong and, since I had become ill in South East Asia, I was sent to Edinburgh Western Infirmary's rare diseases ward.

By this point I resembled a concentration camp survivor with the amount of weight I had lost. After a lot more tests I was diagnosed as having a Strongyloidiasis infection. Caused by roundworm, this disease apparently killed many prisoners of war who were building the bridge and railway on the River Kwai. There was no cure for "strongyloidiasis" back then, but thankfully there is now a tablet that kills the invasive worm. Without the cure it gradually makes it way from your intestine into your vital organs, and by this point you are soon to die. How close I was to departing the scene, I have no idea. After taking the single tablet I started to feel better. I needed a lot of building up, eating good meals and putting some weight back on. After another couple of weeks, I started to even enjoy having a beer again. Through time my clothes started to fit me again.

Once recovered, it was time to get back to South East Asia. Ensco had a surprise waiting for me - and not a good one, I hasten to add. Ensco now hired more and more Americans and it was becoming tedious when visiting any of their rigs to conduct training. They simply did not want the training and looked at this as a complete waste of time and money. I conducted courses firstly onboard the Ensco 108 in Vietnam and, as the rig manager was a South African, the training went without any problems. The next rig, however, was in Lamprell's shipyard in the United Arab Emirates and this was the start of the end. Two of Freddie's instructors were already onboard when I arrived, and I noticed straight away the way these people were treating and speaking to the instructors. It was nothing short of a disgrace. They certainly can drill oil wells, but their man-management skills were deplorable.

One of the courses to be conducted was HLO training, but I could not believe my eyes at what was waiting for us. There were containers and pipe work stored on the helideck, which is a big NO in the industry as the helideck should be used for nothing but landing helicopters. Most rigs are designed so that the cranes cannot reach the helideck, but not in this case. When I spoke politely with the OIM, who hailed from the Deep South, about the safety breach he simply went off on one! My reply was simple, there would be no HLO training until the helideck was cleared and not used as a storage area. As we were in a shipyard there was plenty of space at the quay side for storage.

Ensco had an office in Dubai and the operations manager, who I thought I had a very good business relationship with, was in town from Singapore. He summonsed me to a meeting at their office. At the meeting I was presented with a list of complaints about JCD from USA Ensco employees. This had turned into a witch hunt and it was being orchestrated by the boys from the Deep South. I showed this list of complaints later to the HSE manager, who I had also known from way back when I first went into business, and he could not believe what he was reading. He also made a valid point - if someone had a complaint about you and your training it should have been dealt with immediately, not compiled to make some long list.

We completed the contracted training on board the rig in shipyard, Sharjah UAE, now Sharjah is supposed to be a dry part of UAE (NO Alcohol) when working in the shipyard soon found out that there was indeed a Seaman's Club in the shipyard that sold beer, wine, spirits and tobacco at duty free prices it certainly resembled a duty free shop at an airport, with the training completed and after digesting the long list of complaints against JCD Training decided on a visit to the Seaman's Club and what an absolute brilliant night it turned out to be! There were oil field people from the rigs and seaman from the many ships, people from all over the globe, on one table there were a group of Iraqi seaman and how entertaining they were, first time I had seen guys mix Heineken lager and whisky (in the same glass) for obvious reasons and with the troubles over the years in Iraq was a little apprehensive about joining these guys for a chat, how wrong I was, everyone was very friendly and got along fine it was good atmosphere all the troubles in the strange world we live in today yet here were people from all over the globe sitting in a club in of all places Sharjah in the Middle East having a real good time. Unfortunately all good things come to an end and in the morning that was it. JCD Training were not to be used by

159

Ensco again for training, or until at least the list was addressed. How could you possibly address this list? It was practically impossible. Never get into a battle you cannot win, came to mind. After travelling home and having a good think about the situation I decided that it had been very disappointing to end things like this, but there was a plus side – we wouldn't have to deal with any of these red necks again. Most of the good people I had known from the early days of Ensco had parted company with them anyway.

On checking the contract, it turned out that JCD Training were going to get the last laugh anyway. They had terminated the contract wrongly, so I had a word with my lawyer and he in turn wrote to the Ensco legal team. My case never even went to court as they settled and JCD walked away with a tidy compensation package. Goodbye and good riddance Ensco!

I had Freddie up to speed with crane training and he would be able to conduct any training for us in Vietnam. This was good as it was much easier for Freddie to travel from Malaysia than I from the UK. Freddie was married to a rather large German woman who I can only describe as intelligent enough with a controlling nature. The other instructors were always moaning about her, as she held the purse strings and when these guys were ever travelling the pocket money - as she called it - she gave them for living expenses was nothing short of miserly. The way we had organised the sub-contracting, this had nothing to do with me. Freddie's German wife still held New Zealand residency and one day she asked, with Freddie's permission, for all invoices in the future to be paid into a Kiwi bank account instead of the Malaysian bank. This was fine by me, but it wouldn't be all that long until this came back to bite Freddie.

I sent Freddie and his guys to Myanmar for Seadrill. We had conducted training on the drilling rig, West Trident, before in other parts of Asia, and now it was going to drill two exploration wells in their waters. Local people were going to be hired for the duration which meant a good deal of training was required. Direct flights were not available into Yangon back then - you had to fly through Bangkok. Another problem was that no communications were allowed offshore. While this was an inconvenience for us, it would make the rig manager's job extremely difficult. Myanmar was not the safest place to be, either, because of all the political unrest. On one occasion the rig manager was in a taxi travelling from the airport to his hotel when it was stopped by soldiers. A boy, who was no more than twelve-years-old and dressed in an army uniform, stuck an AK47 assault rifle into the back window of the taxi. In English he asked the rig manager what he was doing in Yangon. I certainly dodged a bullet there, by not travelling. I never let on to Freddie or his guys about the taxi incident. They did report back that the place was very run down, but with being Asian they blended in no problem. From what I remember, they actually enjoyed the trip.

Atwood Oceanic contacted me about training offshore Malabo - the capital of the small oil rich state of Equatorial Guinea in West Africa. The training was to be onboard the Sea Hawk, where I received my back injury in the early 1990s. This ex-Spanish colony is rated as one of the most corrupt places on earth and you can see from its murky past exactly why. Until the discovery of oil this place was just a dot on the map, but the discovery of black gold was to change all that. It was not unlike Brunei in many ways, but much more violent. The money from the oil here wasn't being dispersed into the country's economy and its people, it was instead being pocketed by the ruling family. In a football stadium where the people were having a quiet demonstration about the economy, government troops, on orders from the then president, opened fire. Hundreds of innocent people were slaughtered.

When we arrived, we were taken to a hotel for an overnight stay. This was a full Atwood crew change and personnel were arriving from all over the world. The following morning, we were transported by minibus and land cruisers to the helicopter base. On our way there, we were stopped by soldiers who ordered us at gun point out onto the side of the road, where we had all our passports confiscated. Nobody had a clue what was going on. It was claimed that the soldiers were checking to make sure we were not mercenaries being brought in for a coup.

Strangely my mobile still had a signal, and as I stood beside the minibus it rang. It was my old mate from Selkirk, Elliot 'Ego' Henderson. Without a chance to say anything he launched into...

'The load of logs for your fire is at the entrance to your driveway'.

'The driver can't get access. Are you anywhere nearby to open the gates?'

I explained I was in Africa. We had a good laugh about this many months later. Elliot has a way of calling everyone 'tight' with money. He's a successful forestry contractor, and I'm certainly near the top of his 'tight' list. I wouldn't class him as being tight, but I do remember being in a bar with him one night when he dropped a twenty pence piece. He reacted so quickly in getting down to catch the coin, that it hit him on the back of the head.

Back in Africa, we stood for a considerable time in the heat before one of the officers in charge confirmed we were innocent oil people being taken to the helicopter base to be flown offshore. It later emerged that he had wanted a back hander from the agent to allow us to progress. The agent had to drive back to his office and then the bank to collect the ransom money. It was only when he arrived back, and handed over the cash, that we were free to go on with our journey. It was a relief to finally get to the helicopter base. But, since nobody had turned up for the scheduled flight, it had been cancelled.

We were now to be driven to another port where we would be transported offshore by boat. The joys of the oil industry. This was a frightening experience and another opportunity to weigh up if the business is worth the risks. We were so late in getting offshore all the poor lads heading home had missed their flights and had to stay another night in town before having new air tickets issued. All of this because of a bent officer and worst of all nothing was said.

After finally getting offshore I was encouraged to find a much-changed Sea Hawk. The large crane now had a proper slew ring and pinion, not chain driven as it had been during my previous experience. The old link belt cranes, on the port and starboard sides, had also been replaced by two brand new Sea Trax king post cranes. If, all those years previously, the big crane had been fitted with a proper slew ring and pinion it would have saved one man's life, and my back injury would never have happened.

While we were there the catering crew decided to go on strike. They were all sent back onshore and replaced with a new catering crew. Before the strikers left, one of the cooks who was well-respected by the camp boss, was asked how he would feed his seven children without an income. The guy just simply stood there without saying anything. Later on the camp boss began making some sandwiches to tide us all over until the new catering crew arrived. Much to his surprise, the cook was waiting in the kitchen ready to start work again. When asked why he had changed his mind, he said that he had no intention of going on strike and he'd just gone along with it so that he could get a better cabin once everyone else had been taken off the rig.

I am pleased to say that there were no more dramas during this trip, and everything went to plan. All was well in the office in the UK as well, as my 19-year-old daughter Amy had just started studying Business & Marketing at Heriot Watt University. To help her gain experience, she learned the administration side of our business and this turned out to be good for both parties. Judith continued to do the accounts as usual, while Amy took on the rest of the administration duties.

A new client called Premier Drilling came on board at this time. This company did not own any rigs but just managed and crewed rigs for their owners. Almost all of the Premier Drilling rigs were new, and it was a pleasure to conduct training for them. With these new contracts it was time to hire more Instructors to keep up with the workload. We hired two Indians – a young lad from Mumbai who was originally from Goa, and the other from Chennai, who had an English grandmother. Both of our new instructors had a good command of the English language. I travelled to Mumbai to meet both of them, bring them up to speed on how we conducted courses, and also order work clothes for them. Recruiting the two Indian instructors was a good move.

I received a phone call from Freddie's wife in Malaysia, while he was conducting training in Vietnam, to tell me that one of the Malaysian instructors had died. I knew the chap had been ill, but I did not realise how bad his illness had been. A few minutes later I received a phone call from PVD in Vietnam to say that 'Mr Freddie and his wife' had been into their accounts department requesting an advance of money. I thought, wait a minute, I have just spoken with the woman in Malaysia and now you are saying she is with Freddie in Vietnam? And they are after money? It took a while to realise what was going on, but I had noticed a change in Freddie on a previous assignment. He hadn't been the jovial colleague he usually was. At the time, I had put his mood down to the fact that one of his brothers had passed away. It turned out he had not been getting on at home with his German wife and had taken up with a local woman from Malaysia. This woman had five children to five different men and was still married to a husband who was in a wheelchair. Without telling me, Freddie had flown this woman to Vietnam with him and had her in the training class acting as an assistant. She had left the five children with her disabled husband in Malaysia. Freddie had introduced her to the people at PVD as his wife. When they had spent all their money Freddie had come up with the great idea of asking PVD Training for an advance. This was when they contacted me, as they were unhappy to have been asked.

I was both embarrassed and angry. Once I cooled down, I realised I was left with no alternative than to sack Mr Freddie immediately. It was sad to think that you know someone after working with them for some time, but really you do not know them at all. I felt badly let down as we had travelled to many places together and he was earning money that he would never have made anywhere else. It had been a good working relationship, but I had no option but to end it there and then. Freddie's German wife, who eventually found out about his affair, threw him out of the marital home. She asked if I would carry on with the arrangement of using the Malaysian instructors. I was happy to continue the arrangement with her – but it wasn't all that long until I was to receive another below-the-belt punch, this time from her.

We used to receive numerous enquiries about American Petroleum Institute (API) training. For years I had responded that this was American standard training and, with coming from the UK, we could not deliver the courses. The penny finally dropped with me on this one when speaking with an API representative. The conversation gradually came around to the process of becoming an API approved training provider. It would be time consuming and costly, however, if JCD Training was successful in gaining approval we would be the first non-American company to gain API RP 2D - the American standard for lifting in the oil industry. On the back of this we would be able to conduct courses in offshore crane inspection, offshore crane operator and rigger.

It was decided by API that the audit process was to be a two-part exercise. The first part would be with one of their assessors, onboard a rig in a shipyard in Singapore, on the practical exercises we were going to offer. The other would be a desk top audit at our office in the UK. I contacted Premier Drilling who had a rig in the shipyard in Singapore and was delighted to be given the go-ahead to use their rig cranes. The first part of the audit went very well, as this is what we do every day in our training. The second part however, turned out to be a nightmare. I flew the API auditor up from the South of England to Edinburgh collected him at Edinburgh Airport and drove him to a hotel in Selkirk where he would be staying for the duration. At our office later that day, when he looked at our paperwork, he requested to look at our business management system. The problem was, we simply did not have one!

The auditor, who was booked by us for three days, gave me two options. We could, either, take him back to the airport and bring in a third party to develop a business management system, or we could sit down together and start from scratch. As we had all the information required to produce a business management system, it is just a matter of putting it all together. Talk about burning the candles at both ends, I was still writing at three o'clock the following morning. In all my time in business, I had never thought that we would ever need anything like this, but this management system turned out to be a blessing. Following another two days of inputting procedures and documents covering Control of System, Quality Control, Procedures of Systems, and a Management Manual, it gradually began to come together like a large jigsaw puzzle.

Without the auditor's experience and assistance, we would never have been able to produce a system like this. He was happy with the finished product and everything was then sent to API in Washington DC for their approval. Apart from a couple of requests for some fine-tuning here and there, they were happy with us, and we soon received the welcome news that, in accordance with their Training Provider Course Programme, JCD Training was the first training provider outside of the USA to be a fully approved training provider. With the permission from Seadrill, JCD Training conducted its first API offshore crane inspection course onboard one of their new rigs on board the West Jaya in the shipyard in Singapore. I knew immediately that this course was going to be something special.

It was not long before the enquiries for API training started to overtake anything else we offered. This was mainly because the major oil companies who were now in South East Asia had API RP 2 D as their recognised lifting standard.

We had the Indian Instructors trained to deliver the API offshore crane operator and rigger courses, with me conducting the API offshore crane inspection courses in Singapore. It was going to be a busy time for both of them with the API courses being organised at offshore locations around South East Asia. Thankfully, they could be almost anywhere in that region within four hours from India, and they both enjoyed travelling. There was a setback, though. Just as our API courses were gathering momentum, Premier Drilling went bust. It was an uncertain few weeks, but the owners who took over their own rigs once more opted to continue using us. We were now conducting training courses for Chinese Offshore Services Ltd (COSL) who owned half of the fleet, and Aban Drilling from India, who owned the other half.

The first courses we conducted for Aban and COSL was offshore Iran on Kish Island. It was just off the mainland in the Persian Gulf. Kish Island had been owned for a while by the United Arab Emirates before being returned to Iran. I don't blame them for handing it back – would you want to get into a fight with Iran for ownership of an island? Kish Island was certainly an experience. The clients issued me with a Government of Belize seafarers ID card to ease my passage past immigration on the island. Having a UK passport could have caused problems as there was a blanket ban on anyone from the UK. When arriving on Kish after a flight from Dubai, the immigration for visa processing was a lengthy process. Your fingers were black for days with having so many prints taken for

ID and visa documents. To make matters worse they used the blackest thick ink I had ever seen. There was no soap and water either, just an old rag handed out for anyone who wanted to attempt cleaning their hands.

Prior to the revolution with the Ayatollah coming into power in Iran, Kish had been the luxury holiday destination for the wealthy of the country. But getting offshore to the rig was a problem with next to no helicopters and only boats to take you offshore being regularly hampered by strong winds. Fortune was on my side during my first trip as, when I arrived I was informed that a chopper was available the following day for reaching the rig. The evening before travelling offshore, I had a walk around the place with another guy heading for the rig. One of the locals showed us a large building that was closed. When we looked inside through the dirty windows it had been a casino. You could still see the black-jack and roulette tables coated with inches of dust. It was as if time had stood still when the Shah was deposed. The Ayatollah banned gambling straight away and the doors on the casino hadn't been opened since.

I stayed in a hotel called the Pink Flamingo, which served delicious Persian style food. It is always a treat to dine on this type of food - they certainly know how to cook. I can see why Persian restaurants are so popular. As for the helicopter ride in the morning, well that was a different experience. It was an old Bell 212 - similar to what the USA military used during the Vietnam conflict. Because of all the sanctions on Iran by the USA, helicopter parts must be hard to come by. I have never been so frightened during a helicopter journey in all my life. We had a military armed guard in the chopper for security. I had no idea why we needed security as we weren't leaving Iranian waters to reach the rig. It was a case of shake, rattle and roll as the engine continually threatened to cut out. Helicopters are always noisy, but this was reaching extreme decibels. You could tell the pilot was not comfortable either, as he continued flying very low across the ocean. If anything happened, it was obvious he was ready to ditch into the sea.

I have never been so pleased to see an oil rig in my life. After landing on the deck and my hasty exit, I'm sure I let out a 'phew'. I found out later that day that the chopper ditched on a small

Island on its way back to shore. I believe that was the last helicopter ride to have taken place to rigs in Iran as they simply did not have the parts to keep them safely in the air. Everything was going to be by boat transfer after that - weather permitting. The crews were mostly Indian with a sprinkling of Brits, Australians and Canadians. With Aban and COSL both having a rig in the region it turned out that I was going to make a future visit to the area. As long as it was not by helicopter, it did not bother me.

It was strange looking at the rigs through binoculars from the Iranian side. I had been to the Persian Gulf many times over the years but always viewed the rigs and platforms from the other side of the sea. I noticed platform legs sticking up from waves not all that far from where we were, and enquired if this was new and being prepared for the top side. I was shocked to be told that this had been a platform during the Iraq/Iran conflict. The Iraqis had blown the platform to pieces and after it burned itself out, the top had fallen from its legs into the sea. There were no warning buoys or anything like that to warn shipping that they were passing the remains of an oil platform! For me, this was a disaster waiting to happen as oil tankers are moving in the area both night and day.

The training of the offshore crane operators was soon completed, and all planning in place for other Instructors to take over. It was time for the boat journey back onshore and the flight from Kish to Dubai then onto the UK.

My next and final visit to Iran was much the same as last time except the weather was too bad for boat travel. It was a matter of just sitting around at the hotel waiting on the weather to improve. Thank goodness the World Cup was on the TV even although the commentator was Iranian, speaking excitedly in their native Persian or Farsi tongue. It was far too hot to go for a walk through the day, but I always enjoyed an evening walk once the temperatures cooled. Once again, because of the embargos and sanctions, there was not an awful lot to see in the shops. In one window of a sports shop they had a tiger's paw for sale? At first I thought it was a fancy glove of some kind, but unfortunately the paw was real. Where this had come from, I have no idea but this was the real thing and was for sale!

After sitting around for five days, the oil company decided it was safe enough for the boat ride to the rig. This journey was certainly not as scary as the helicopter ride, but the further we went offshore the worse the sea became. Eventually the captain decided enough was enough and, in broken English, he informed us he was turning back. It was to be another two days before finally getting offshore. Once I had my side of the project finally completed, it was going to be over to the Indian Instructors to return and complete the training on both the rigs. They were certainly going to be made a lot more welcome than a UK passport holder. You never really felt safe in Iran and I am pleased that at least we never had to go onto the mainland for visa processing.

JCD Training was provisionally booked to conduct offshore crane operator training onboard West Atlas, offshore Australia. But the job was hastily cancelled due to the rig taking a massive kick, a 'blow out'. There were some strange circumstances surrounding this blow out as the rig was almost completely destroyed and the oil spill turned out to be Australia's third largest spill. There had been six previous blow outs in Australian waters, between 1965 and 1984, but this was by far the worst. Seadrill's emergency response team was commended on how they conducted the abandonment plan, with all sixty-nine personnel safely evacuated.

The blow out had melted the rig over the platform and until a relief well was successfully drilled, anything from five-hundred to fifteen-hundred barrels was spilling into the sea every day for eleven weeks. After speaking to some of the crew who were involved, and now transferred to other Seadrill rigs, the whole disaster turned out to be what was yet again another industry cock up. There had been a botched up cement job to start with, pressure tests had not been carried out on a well that had previous troubles, and all work had been suspended on the well the previous year because of problems with secondary safety devices. Pressure containing anti corrosion caps had not been fitted on one casing, and while one had been fitted to the other casing section, it had never been tested.

This was incompetent higher management yet again. There were people making very poor statements at the enquiry, no doubt to try and cover their mistakes and cover their backs by trying to pass the blame on. This rig was a recipe for disaster, and it was only by the good work of the emergency response team that no one was injured or killed. As for the environment, the damage must have been immense to both aquatic and shore life, even if the field is a good way out at sea. Despite the scale of the environmental disaster, the media coverage of the enquiry was limited. Maybe if people had been killed, they would have taken a greater interest.

After a good break at home it was time for another trip to Singapore. After contacting KCA Deutag about possibly conducting an API offshore crane inspection course onboard one of their old barges in the shipyard it was Singapore here we come. Around this time we also met an accountant to arrange setting up JCD Training (Singapore) Pte Ltd. We were paying far too much tax in the UK and with tax rates not near as high in Singapore, we decided we could offset this against our UK accounts.

The API offshore crane inspection course aboard the KCA barge was another success. With JCD Training (Singapore) Pte Ltd now a proper registered company we applied for my Singapore employment pass. This is a great card to hold, especially at passport control. You simply walk forward to the Singapore Citizens gates, missing all the large cues at immigration. There is the added advantage of no passport stamps, keeping valuable passport pages clean.

We needed a permanent home for this training as it looked like we would be conducting between six and eight courses every year. Through a friend of a friend, I was introduced to a shipyard out by the Tuas area on the west side of the island, quite close to the causeway over to Malaysia. It was a perfect location for a course of this nature with the shipyard having many cranes, two suitable classrooms, use of toilets, a changing area, and also canteen facilities for lunches and breaks. The only real problem at this early stage was getting out from the city in the morning and back in the evenings. It was quickly decided to conduct a course and see how this would work. Thankfully, everyone involved considered the initial course as a success. The canteen facilities were not the best and transport was an issue, but gradually we found an outside caterer and, although we could not pick up everyone in the mornings, we hired a transport company with a people carrier to bring every one into the city at the end of the day. All the participants had to do themselves was to make their own way out to shipyard in the morning.

When in Singapore I always stayed at the Pan Pacific Hotel on Orchard. I had stayed at this hotel many times over the years when it was known as the Negara Hotel. It was central and suited me to the ground. I ended up practically a permanent fixture there, and the staff and management treated me like royalty. It was very much home from home.

Good old Eddie McWilliams was also in Singapore at this time. Eddie had been made redundant by Transocean and landed the attractive post as training and QHSE manager with Aban Drilling, who we had already carried out courses for in crane operator training. Eddie was based full time in Singapore and, after some of his posts with Transocean, he had taken to his new surroundings like a duck to water. We often met for drinks and a chat about the old days. Eddie also came to my rescue when the Singapore Grand Prix was on. His family were back in Scotland and he was living in a massive company apartment on his own. I hadn't checked the dates of my next course and it coincided with the formula one race. Every hotel in Singapore was almost fully booked and the few remaining rooms had ridiculous prices. I was left with an option of either cancelling the course or ask Eddie for a bed. He was more than happy with the company as it was going to be sometime before any of his family moved over. We came up with the permanent arrangement for me to stay at his apartment any time I was in Singapore until his family relocated.

It was brilliant at night-time as we were just a five-minute walk from the popular Holland Village with all its bars and eating places. No traffic is allowed in the area in the evenings either, making the pedestrian-only walk all the more enjoyable. If we did not fancy anything substantial to eat there was always the hawker stands at Holland Village - cheap and cheerful food to suit any nationality.

In the days before and after the Grand Prix being staged in Singapore, I noticed a significant increase in the number of road accidents. I can only assume that the commuters in the mornings thought they were Lewis Hamilton. On one morning, my journey from the city to the shipyard, which normally takes between half an hour and forty-five minutes, took more than two hours with all the lane closures and diversions due to accidents.

As the shipyard now had vessels coming in and out all the time, we were now in the strong position of being able to offer API rigger and offshore crane operator training courses. Everything was falling into place and the price of oil was high and almost every rig was operational. Then, out of the blue, I received a call from API to see if I knew anything about a Malaysian company that had submitted an application to become a training provider using almost identical paperwork to our own. I obtained the application number and phoned Freddie's, now, ex-wife. Initially she tried to deny any knowledge of the application, before launching into some cock and bull story about needing API for some work in Malaysia.

'If that was the case, why not come and speak with me beforehand?' I enquired.

If she had talked to me about doing training off their own backs in Malaysia I doubt I would have bothered about it, but to go behind my back like this was the final straw. Firstly, I had Freddie and his new lady friend going behind my back in the PVD training room, and now this. Being honest, with Freddie not being on the scene anymore, all the good Malaysian instructors had moved on due to the way the German woman spoke to and treated them. A short time after I had ended the business venture with the Malaysians, I found out that Freddie was back living in the Sarawak city of Miri. Unsurprisingly, the German ex-wife had been making sure all the money had been going to New Zealand, leaving him with nothing. I was also told that Freddie had planted rubber trees on the land he owned near Miri just before we parted company. The idea was to start harvesting rubber when the trees were mature to provide a regular income. He had seemingly bought very expensive saplings from Thailand, but they were never properly looked after and the whole lot died. I have never seen or heard of Freddie again, nor, I'm pleased to say, his German ex-wife.

With the Indian instructors taking care of the offshore training and yours truly settled into the new shipyard training centre in

Singapore, as well as Judith and Amy taking care of the office in UK, things were sailing along smoothly. As the saying goes, 'make hay while the sun shines' and this we did for a few years until the dark clouds began gathering again. In the oil industry, troubles are usually on the horizon. The Singapore shipyard fleet operations manager was a great guy called Steve Church, from New Zealand. I had known Steve for a little while by this time and it came as a bitter blow when he revealed that, during a routine health check, he had been diagnosed with an aggressive and advanced cancer. Steve passed away not long after.

It was around Steve's death that the oil industry took a dive. The price of oil was starting to fall rapidly, some would say it collapsed. It quickly became obvious the industry was heading for a serious recession. Rigs were being laid up by the week, and personnel were losing their jobs left, right and centre. The rigs that survived, and were still out working, couldn't generate the attractive day rates they had been making just a few months earlier. As in most sectors, the first budget to be tightened when there is a recession is training. Thankfully, it's illegal to have offshore crane operators onboard a rig without a certificate of competence. While the other courses were suffering, offshore crane training remained steady.

My son, Iain, had started to make noises about joining the industry around this time. For many years it looked as though he would make it as a full-time athlete after enjoying success over 200 metre and 400 metre sprints. However, a knee injury sustained while playing rugby led to three operations and brought an end to his running. Much to his mother's disgust he had also postponed – then cancelled - his place at university to study physics. To start with he learned the administration side of the business and took over as Amy had graduated and taken a job in banking. He enjoyed a break with mates in Australia before coming to meet me in Singapore and so began the process of teaching Iain to become an inspector.

The OIM of a Seadrill rig in the West Lima shipyard came from Hawick – a town just twelve miles along the road from our hometown of Selkirk in Scotland – so getting permission to bring Iain onboard with me wasn't a problem. Iain stayed with me at Eddie's – something I have always been grateful to Eddie for -

and he did well on the many courses he took part in. Although the industry was struggling, Iain secured a position with National Oil Well Varco (NOV) in the Middle East. This is where his learning curve really began. I'm pleased to say that after gaining plenty experience, he went it alone and began freelancing as an inspector. Douglas Inspection Ltd was born and continues to do well with Iain plying his trade all over the world as an offshore inspector.

The recession was biting hard for our company with training offshore practically non-existent month after month. The downturn meant we had to unfortunately say goodbye to our two Indian instructors. We were keeping our heads above the water with the training at Tuas in Singapore. But API were about to bring even this to an end. With API we were regulated as a Training Programme Course Provider (TPCP), which is an excellent standard, and to meet the criteria you were audited every three years to ensure all was above board. In the background, we had always wanted API to hold a dual qualification for offshore crane inspectors and offshore crane operators. This meant that instead of just following the USA standards we wanted to also introduce the UK lifting standards to provide inspectors and operators with a dual qualification that would be recognised the world over. This would also allow inspectors to work anywhere. But these plans didn't meet approval or any understanding from the API staff in the USA. The final hammer blow came when they decided to scrap the TPCP programme and all of the approved training providers were to be moved over to API University. That was achievable, but they also wanted twenty percent royalties on everything we made. This was in the middle of the worst downturn the industry had ever experienced. I tried for close to a year to see if I could make this work, but can you imagine knocking on someone's door and providing them with a quote before adding a further twenty percent on for the API royalties.

I spoke with the Lifting Equipment Engineers Association (LEEA) from the UK and a meeting was organised in Singapore to see if we could become a member and a training provider. Because we were a training company rather than an inspection firm we didn't meet the requirements for becoming a full member. But they would be happy to welcome us as associate members. They also agreed to carry out an audit with a view to us becoming an accredited LEEA training provider for offshore crane inspection and offshore crane operator. LEEA were also interested in my plans for a dual qualification by meeting US and UK regulations. I resigned from API and moved all of JCD Training over to LEEA. It was, in many ways, sad to leave API but to move across to the API University would never have worked for us. The move to LEEA was a good one, and we are still with them to this day.

With the industry now into a deep recession, looking back it still surprises me how we managed to continue operating at a profit. As we now had no instructors and the possibility of getting ill again was at the back of my mind, I decided to offer Eddie the opportunity of becoming, through JCD Training, a registered Instructor with LEEA. Thankfully, Eddie liked the idea. Being honest, the courses were old hat to someone of Eddie's experience. Another Scots lad who had been through our training courses in the past was Darryl Fury. Darryl was now married and living in the Philippines. When I approached him about a similar part-time arrangement like we had with Eddie, he was also interested in joining us.

Darryl flew over to Singapore for a five-day Train the Trainer course – which he passed with flying colours. We worked out that between the three of us, we had more than one hundred years of experience in the oil industry. That is something you cannot buy. Eddie agreed to take care of any little jobs at the weekends or when he was on a holiday, while Darryl would make himself available whenever he had time off. With Darryl living in Asia he was closer at hand as well for most of the contracts.

The introduction of Eddie and Darryl was good for business. Not only were they good at their jobs, it was satisfying to have such experienced people to run things past. Eddie's family were relocating from the UK meaning there is no way I would overstay my welcome at his apartment. I moved back to the Pan Pacific Hotel during my stays in Singapore. I am not sure who they thought was returning to the hotel, but on one of my first stays back at the hotel you would have thought I was royalty or a VIP. The staff continually upgraded me to a suite with all the perks.

On one occasion the welcoming card in my room, accompanied with a lovely bowl of fruit and chocolates, made me laugh.

'Welcome home Air Commander Douglas' it read.

Where they got the idea that I was an air commander still baffles me, but the hotel had great staff and it made my time there feel like a home from home. The hotel has recently been demolished and Pan Pacific are in the process of building a replacement. I am wondering if Air Commander Douglas will be invited to the opening. Judith and I were at a wedding of a Singapore friend not long ago and we stayed at the other Pan Pacific over by Marina Bay. Most of the staff had been transferred from Pan Pacific Orchard to work there until new hotel is built, and once again when checking in we were overwhelmed by the welcome we received.

Unfortunately for Eddie, not long after this Aban Drilling made him redundant and he was left with no alternative but to move back home to the UK following his ninety days' notice. Worse was to come for our Singapore operations as the shipyard at Tuas, where we were based, closed their doors. This left JCD Training with no training venue. It had been noticeable for a while leading up to the closure as the shipyard was gradually becoming quieter, and the staff numbers had diminished. However, we were not given any notice of the sudden closure. We knew the parent company who owned the shipyard was in severe financial difficulties, but we did not anticipate a closure. Where all the money had disappeared to from the golden days not all that long before appears a mystery, but these people are like magicians when it comes to making money disappear! One story was that the parent company borrowed Sing$350 million dollars from a local government bank. Two weeks later they applied to go into liquidation and the Sing$350 million disappeared. Directors were arrested and released on huge bail payments, but for the most part whatever happened has been swept under the carpet.

Was this time for me to may be call it a day? The thought certainly went through my head. I contemplated continuing JCD Training (Singapore) Pte Ltd but what was the point in keeping a Singapore company when the chances of generating business there was diminishing by the month. I decided to wind up JCD (Singapore) Pte Ltd.

It was around this time that I received an email then phone call from PVD Training Vietnam. Following the Freddie fiasco, these were the last people I expected to hear from. We arranged a meeting in Vung Tau and it was enjoyable to catch up with the PVD Training staff again. With JCD Training still having training provider licences and instructors, it was proposed that we go into a joint venture with PVD. Their training centre had come on leaps and bounds, and they also had a rig, the PVD5, stacked in the harbour for all our practical exercises. They would bring their clients to the table and I bring mine.

A deal was struck, and suddenly we were back in business. I'm pleased to say that more than three years down the road this joint venture is still going strong and I enjoy my little jaunts down to Vietnam. It's a different place to when I first visited all those years earlier.

Eddie and Darryl still conduct part time training for JCD Training. Darryl conducts quite a few of the courses in Vung Tau while Eddie covers all of Europe.

Eddie also visited a platform in the Ivory Coast for us to conduct refresher offshore crane operator courses. The crew here had been using one side of the platform as a toilet due to the condition of the old toilet. The OIM onboard had decided to have the old toilets ripped out and refurbished. While Eddie was there, one of course-participants had painted the walls and assisted in hanging the doors of the new toilets. The job had been completed and the new toilets were working, but Eddie noticed his participant had disappeared just before class was to start. Eddie waited for about ten minutes when the man eventually returned, he was asked where he had been.

'I just went to the toilet' came his reply.

It turned out that, even though the new toilets were working, he and the other crew were still using the side of the platform for relieving themselves.

Darryl had a lot more to worry about than toilets during a trip to Mexico. He was lucky to live to tell the tale. He was working onboard a Pipe Laying Vessel (PLV) called the Sampson on an eight-weeks on, eight-weeks off rotation. This suited us perfectly as he could conduct training courses during his eight weeks off. The vessel was at anchorage, some ten miles offshore from Ciudad Del Carmen. At around 9pm one Saturday evening the captain on the bridge was getting ready to wind down, along with his three officers, when he noticed a vessel approaching at speed. It was only pirates! We're not talking about a bunch of scallywags led by a guy with a wooden leg and a patch over his eye here, these guys are well-equipped and organised with military precision. Although it's not widely reported in the media, Mexican waters are rife with these attacks. It wasn't that long before this incident that pirates had attacked a platform and scaled up the legs to get onboard.

The alarm was sounded from the bridge and the crew headed for the citadel, which is a designated safe area. Crews practise this drill in accordance with maritime rules. Meanwhile, the captain and his three officers barricaded themselves into the large bridge area. Both entrances – the stern and aft – were closed off. The pirates boarded the Sampson and began looting all the cabins. Darryl and his crew mates in the citadel were trying to raise the alarm by calling onshore. Although the lines are supposed to be manned round-the-clock in case of emergencies, nobody was picking up. Eventually one of the guys, who knew the girl from the company's office in Glasgow, managed to contact her on her mobile. She was having a drink in a pub on a Sunday lunch time when she took the call that pirates were raiding the PLV. Having looted the crew's possessions from the cabins, the pirates were now trying t break into the bridge. After a few failed attempts they opened fire on the windows with their semi-automatic weapons. The captain managed to avoid the bullets and debris by diving over a couch. He and his three officers then made their getaway from the bridge to a nearby thruster room and they again barricaded themselves in.

Inside the bridge the pirates ransacked the place and took anything of value. It was fortunate that they never captured anyone on board as they would have beaten them close to death until the citadel door was opened. As well as looting the cabins they set fire to some of the curtains and bedding. By this time, the girl in a Glasgow pub had alerted the Mexican authorities, who in turn dispatched their navy. The pirates, anticipating the

178

alarm will be raised at some point, have someone on shore watching for the navy to leave port. The signal must have been sent that the navy was on its way as they quickly fled in their boats.

Darryl rightfully pointed out that the pirates have inside information about when vessels are anchored, where they are, and who's on board. Who provides the information is anyone's guess as the agents know, the police know and the navy is also told of all rig and vessel movements.

While Darryl was hiding from machine-gun shooting pirates, I received an invitation to conduct an Inspection course in Trinidad for a small company called DG Inspection Services. They were owned by a local chap called Dave Gajadhar. He also wanted me to meet all the majors in Trinidad when I was there to see if any further business could be developed. The course went well. I used Dave's office for a classroom and cranes were available nearby at the Chaguaramas shipyard for practical exercises. But the Port of Spain is not a place for the nervous. Gang warfare is rife and when I was there a teacher sent a small boy home from school because he had a hole in the knee of his trousers. As the poor lad walked home to change, he was caught up in crossfire between two gangs. He died from a stray bullet.

Darryl's experience in Mexico took me back to a story my good friend at Manchester City FC, Bernard Halford, told me. City had signed a Mexican player and when it was time for him to be sold on, Bernard contacted the player and his agent to inform them that if they waited for six to eight weeks for their money they would be exempt from VAT. It was around six-to-eight weeks later that Bernard instructed the accounts department to transfer the six-figure sum that was due over to the agent. A few more weeks passed when Bernard received an alarming call from the player asking where the money was. When Bernard informed him that money had been paid to the agent, he was called a liar and warned never to visit Mexico as he would be shot. After some investigating, it turned out that the agent had done a runner with the entire fee. It would seem corruption is rife in Mexico, whether it's football agents, shipping agents or even the authorities.

As for the PLV Sampson, once the pirates had fled the captain gave the order for the vessel to lift anchor and make its way to Freetown in the Bahamas. On arrival the crew decided enough was enough and most of them decided it was time to call it a day. As for Darryl he headed back to the Philippines and after recovering from the shock of the pirate attack he returned to conducting training for us in Vietnam.

By this point it should have been... and they lived happily ever after. But the oil industry, like every other sector, has been hit terribly by the coronavirus pandemic. Almost everyone has spent most of the year in some form of lockdown, and all of our courses in Vietnam have been cancelled or postponed. It would seem the rollercoaster I boarded in 1987 has a few more twists and turns in store for me yet. But I do know once we have the pandemic conquered myself, Darryl and Eddie will be back in the classroom trying to make the oil industry that little bit safer. As for my venture with PVD Training, hopefully it will continue until January of 2023 when I will turn sixty-six-years-old – and I can perhaps enjoy a well-earned retirement.